FRANCIS FRITH'S

MARKET HARBOROUGH - A HISTORY AND CELEBRATION

THE FRANCIS FRITH COLLECTION

www.francisfrith.com

MARKET HARBOROUGH

A HISTORY AND CELEBRATION
OF THE TOWN

MATT HOWLING

Produced by The Francis Frith Collection

www.francisfrith.com

First published in the United Kingdom in 2004 by
The Francis Frith Collection®

Hardback Edition 2004 ISBN 1-90493-838-8
Paperback Edition 2012 ISBN 978-1-84589-646-1

British Library Cataloguing in Publication Data

Market Harborough - A History and Celebration of the Town
Matt Howling

The Francis Frith Collection®
Oakley Business Park, Wylye Road,
Dinton, Wiltshire SP3 5EU
Tel: +44 (0) 1722 716 376
Email: info@francisfrith.co.uk
www.francisfrith.com

Printed and bound in Great Britain
Contains material sourced from responsibly managed forests

Front Cover: **MARKET HARBOROUGH, THE SQUARE 1922** 72264t

Additional photographs by Matt Howling
Domesday extract used in timeline by kind permission of
Alecto Historical Editions, www.domesdaybook.org.
Aerial photographs reproduced under licence from
Simmons Aerofilms Limited.
Historical Ordnance Survey maps reproduced under licence from
Homecheck.co.uk

*The colour-tinting in this book is for illustrative purposes only,
and is not intended to be historically accurate*

AS WITH ANY HISTORICAL DATABASE, THE FRANCIS FRITH ARCHIVE IS
CONSTANTLY BEING CORRECTED AND IMPROVED, AND THE PUBLISHERS
WOULD WELCOME INFORMATION ON OMISSIONS OR INACCURACIES

Contents

MARKET HARBOROUGH, OLD GRAMMAR SCHOOL 1922 72269p

Historical Timeline for Market Harborough

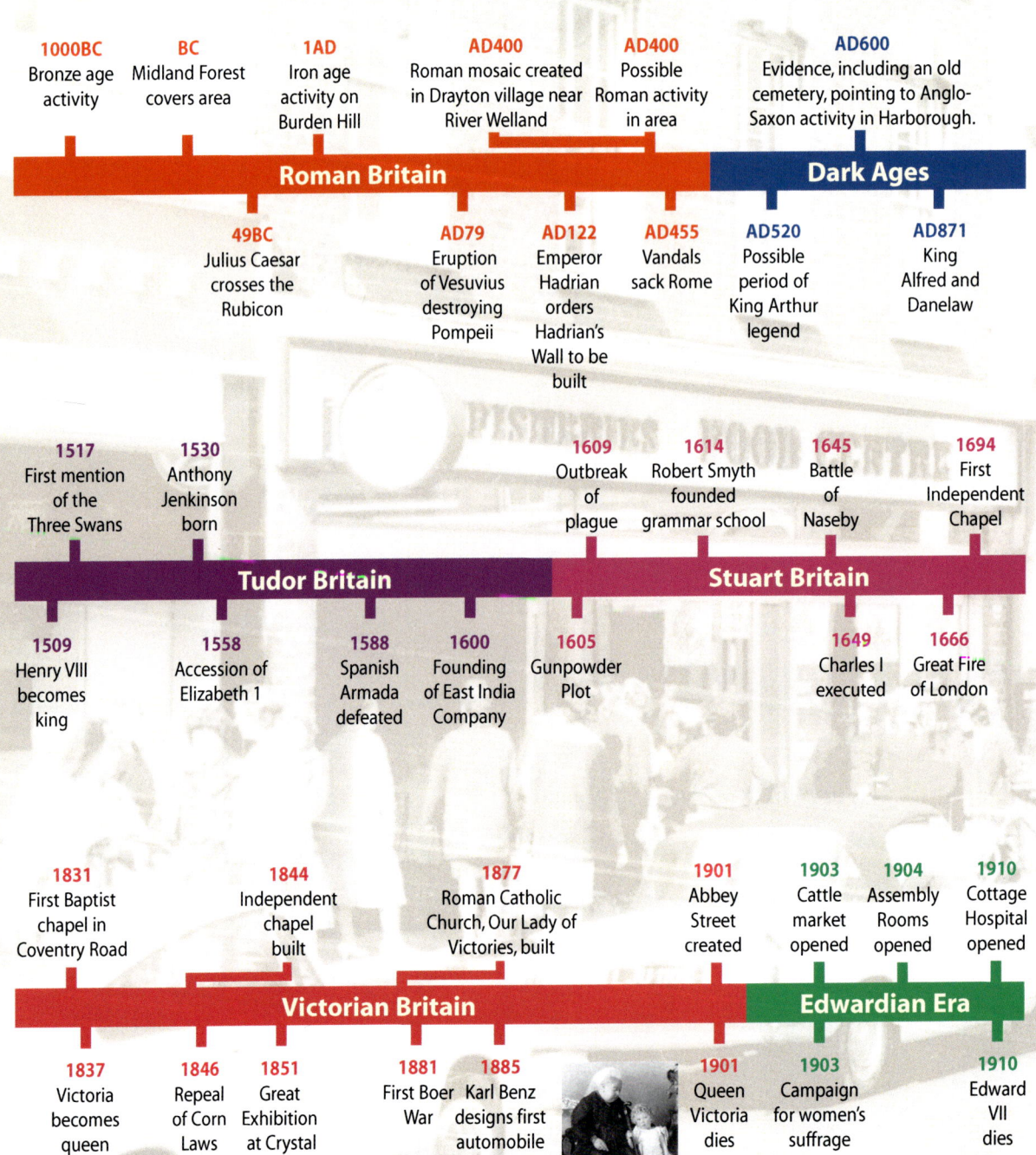

1000BC
Bronze age activity

BC
Midland Forest covers area

1AD
Iron age activity on Burden Hill

AD400
Roman mosaic created in Drayton village near River Welland

AD400
Possible Roman activity in area

AD600
Evidence, including an old cemetery, pointing to Anglo-Saxon activity in Harborough.

Roman Britain

Dark Ages

49BC
Julius Caesar crosses the Rubicon

AD79
Eruption of Vesuvius destroying Pompeii

AD122
Emperor Hadrian orders Hadrian's Wall to be built

AD455
Vandals sack Rome

AD520
Possible period of King Arthur legend

AD871
King Alfred and Danelaw

1517
First mention of the Three Swans

1530
Anthony Jenkinson born

1609
Outbreak of plague

1614
Robert Smyth founded grammar school

1645
Battle of Naseby

1694
First Independent Chapel

Tudor Britain

Stuart Britain

1509
Henry VIII becomes king

1558
Accession of Elizabeth 1

1588
Spanish Armada defeated

1600
Founding of East India Company

1605
Gunpowder Plot

1649
Charles I executed

1666
Great Fire of London

1831
First Baptist chapel in Coventry Road

1844
Independent chapel built

1877
Roman Catholic Church, Our Lady of Victories, built

1901
Abbey Street created

1903
Cattle market opened

1904
Assembly Rooms opened

1910
Cottage Hospital opened

Victorian Britain

Edwardian Era

1837
Victoria becomes queen

1846
Repeal of Corn Laws

1851
Great Exhibition at Crystal Palace

1881
First Boer War

1885
Karl Benz designs first automobile

1901
Queen Victoria dies

1903
Campaign for women's suffrage begins

1910
Edward VII dies

1180
King Henry II grants Manor of Bowden and Harborough to William Mauduit

1336-1370
Harborough's parish church built and October Fair started.

1490-1500
First bequest to the Town Estate

Middle Ages · Late Medieval

1066
Battle of Hastings. Norman rule begins

1086
Domesday Book

1170
Murder of Thomas à Becket at Canterbury cathedral

1215
Magna Carta

1306
Robert the Bruce declares himself King of Scotland

1348
Black Death kills 25 million in Europe

1415
Battle of Agincourt

1485
Battle of Bosworth Field marks end of Plantaganet dynasty

1735
Harborough church spire blown off in a tempest

1768
King of Denmark passes through town

1788
Town Hall built

1809
Canal reaches Harborough

Georgian Era

1739
John Wesley founds Methodist church

1762
Mozart performs at the age of 6

1789
French Revolution

1815
Battle of Waterloo

1825
Stockton to Darlington Railway

1928
New Northampton Road bridge built

1935
Official opening of Welland Park

1959
Commons Car Park created

1983
Harborough Museum opened

20th Century Britain

1914
First World War begins

1926
John Logie Baird obtains first television picture

1939
Outbreak of Second World War

1956
Suez Crisis

1966
England win World Cup

1969
First man on the Moon

1982
Falklands Conflict

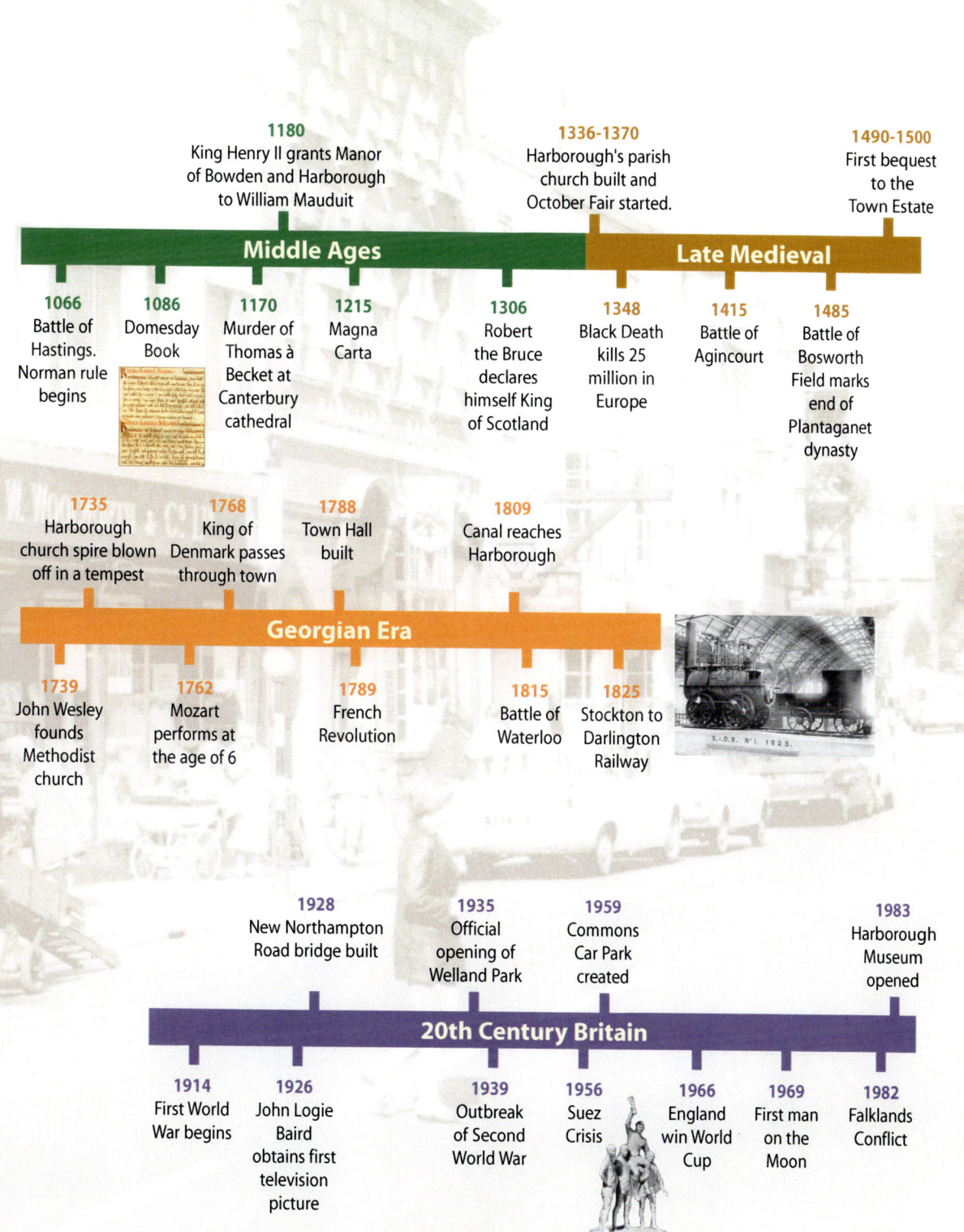

CHAPTER ONE

From Nothing to Something

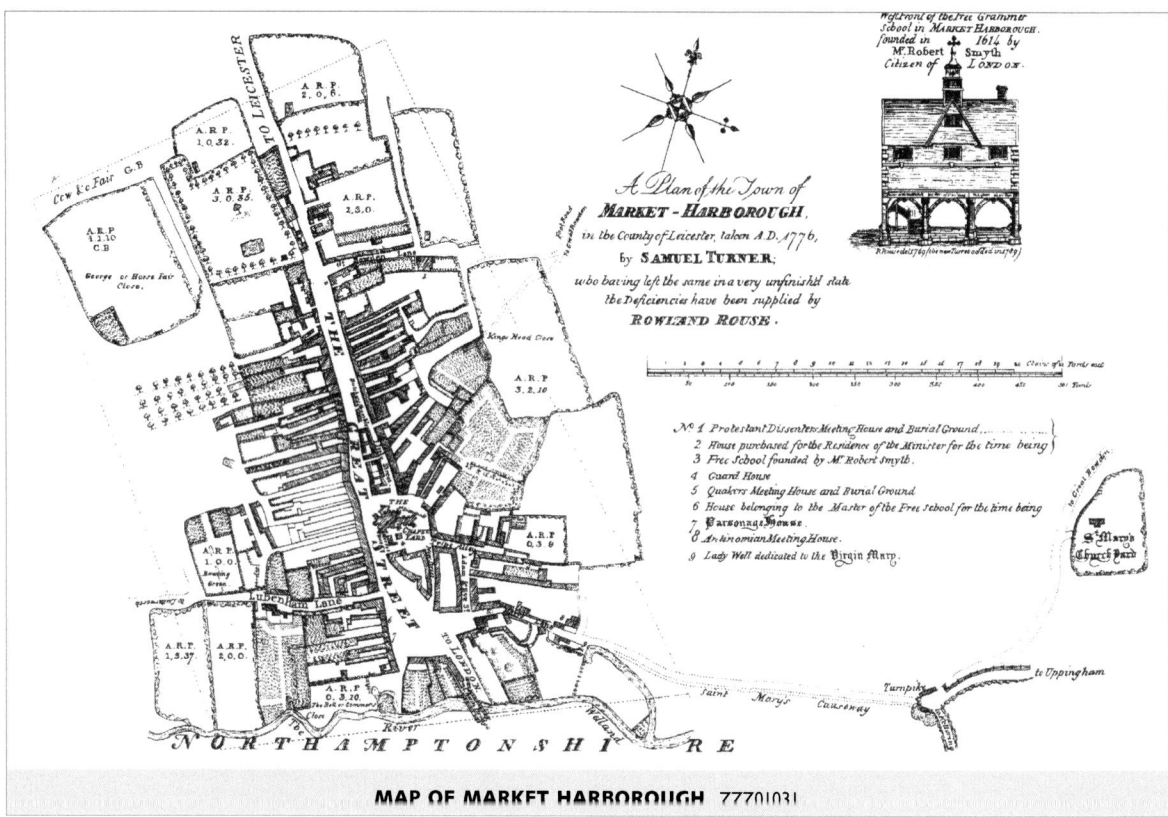

MAP OF MARKET HARBOROUGH 77701031

FROM ITS HUMBLE BEGINNINGS as a medieval New Town to the vibrant, bustling town of today, Market Harborough is a place rich in character, rich in history and rich in community. You only have to take a brief stroll around the town centre to discover a thriving, friendly community, as welcoming as any in Britain and to be a Harborian is to be incredibly proud of your links with the town. But even adopted Harborians, who have moved to the town from elsewhere, develop an uncanny sense of belonging.

Market Harborough has often been described as the gem of Leicestershire - a bold statement, agreed, but one supported by a wealth of breathtaking architecture. The town centre is one of the most picturesque in the country, with its towering parish church spire and quaint 17th-century grammar school: striking landmarks which Harborians often take for granted. It is the town's architectural assets and its uncanny sense of period which continues to intrigue visitors year after year. It is a town which lies deep in the rich pasture land of the Welland Valley, surrounded by small, attractive villages. Its river, the Welland, was once a county border separating Leicestershire and Northamptonshire. Nowadays, walkers enjoy the picturesque stroll along its banks.

As its the name suggests, the town was founded as a purpose-built market town in the 1150s. It has attracted visitors for hundreds of years, a trend which continues to this day. As well as embracing the new, Market Harborough has managed to retain the character of the old. In fact, you only have to glance around for striking clues about the town's historical roots. Market Harborough is a town shaped by its past. The vibrant, bustling community of today has grown out of centuries of change - environmentally, socially and economically, and its history is as colourful as the town is today.

The first ever mention of Market Harborough appears to be in the Beauchamp Cartulary for 7 July 1153. The name Harborough derives from the Anglo-Saxon Haefera-beorg meaning 'the hill where oats are grown'. It was the name of a field used by the men of Bowden and Arden, which is now Mill Hill. The town has also been known as Haverbergam, and would later, of course, become Harborough. Although Harborough is a relatively new town in historical terms, there is evidence that people have been in the area for more than 4,000 years. Archaeological finds in the River Welland date back that far, long before Market Harborough existed, but it seems that people did not start to stay until much later.

There are theories that a huge expanse of dense forest and swampland covered the area in ancient times - part of what is known as the Midland Forest. The forest, dominated by oak trees, would have emerged about 10,000 years ago after the last Ice Age. Wild animals such as cattle, deer and pigs would have roamed in its midst. Bears and wolves may have inhabited the woods too. This thick forest would have made it almost impossible for people to penetrate the area and settle and would have offered little in the way of food. But intriguing evidence of scattered pottery, ditches, enclosures and flint working sites suggests some Bronze and Iron Age settlements.

Bronze Age pottery urns, dating back 3,000 years, have been found on the site which is now the Logan Street Recreation Ground. This suggests the presence of a primitive cemetery, as it would have been custom back in those days to burn the dead and put the ashes in urns.

Anyone choosing to settle in the rather inhospitable landscape which dominated at this time would have probably survived on corn and domestic animals for food or hunted wildlife in the forest.

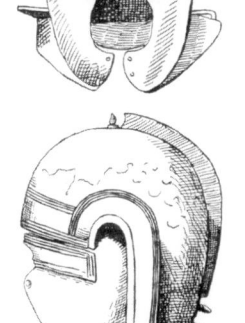

ROMAN HELMET
F6014

The first proper settlement in the area was possibly in the centre of Great Bowden, because the lie of the land would be so suitable. Another theory is that there could have been an early settlement on or around Bowden Hill, along the top of the area that is now covered by the Ridgeway.

If these early settlements did exist they would only have been very primitive hamlets, with perhaps a clearing for a cornfield. Other findings indicate the existence of an important bridge over the River Welland, which is still there today in Northampton Road.

The Romans marched into the area up the Gartree Road from Colchester, which enters the area at Medbourne where it crosses the River Welland into modern Leicestershire. In Harborough Museum today you can see evidence of what is thought to be Roman pottery found near the Ridgeway, where an early settlement could have been. But even at the pinnacle of Roman prosperity in Britain, it is unlikely they ventured into and settled in vast numbers in the Midland Forest.

No reference is made to Market Harborough in the famous land survey of England known as the Domesday Book, prepared on the orders of William the Conqueror after the Norman Conquest in 1066. Why? Because Harborough did not exist at that time. The book does, however, refer to the neighbouring village of Bugedone - now Great Bowden.

A NORMAN SHIP F6019

GREAT BOWDEN, THE VILLAGE 1922 72275

The village of Great Bowden where Market Harborough is thought to have originated. The pond has been filled in. It stood outside a blacksmith's shop. The village church is visible in the background and on the right is a branch of the grocers Symingtons and Thwaites, which also had a shop in Harborough High Street.

GREAT BOWDEN SIGN ZZZ01055

As Bowden expanded, there was a need to create an offshoot development to assist in the management of more distant land. The village of Arden may have assumed this purpose and helped create land in the west where Harborough grew later. Harborough itself is thought to have begun as a 60-acre plot of land laid out in the parish of Great Bowden which spread and developed out of the adjoining villages of Great Bowden, Little Bowden and the now all but vanished settlement of Arden.

ST MARY IN ARDEN CHURCH ZZZ01054

This photo shows the ruins of the unusual St Mary in Arden Church. The church, which collapsed many years ago, stood in the now vanished village of Arden - one of the villages that eventually grew into Harborough. The gravestone in the foreground is that of William Hubbard.

Did you know?

William Hubbard's Legacy

Every year a traditional ceremony is held over William Hubbard's grave in the grounds of St Mary in Arden Church. Hubbard was a gardener who died in 1786. He left the sum of one guinea (£1.05) a year, forever, to the singers of Market Harborough Church on condition that they sang a hymn every Easter Eve over his grave.

One of the last people to be buried in the graveyard was W B Bragg who ran a chemist on the corner of St Mary's Road and Adam and Eve Street. The shop is now a jewellers.

The ruins of the medieval St Mary of Arden chapel, built during the 12th century, can still be seen today at the bottom of Great Bowden Road near the station. The tower collapsed in about 1660, after a long period of neglect, and destroyed the rest of the building. Legend has it that some of the stone was used to help build Welland House, now the Market Harborough Building Society, on the Square. Today all that survives of the original church is the south doorway and the porch. Around the doorway arch you can still see 22 beak-heads. It was rebuilt in the late 17th century and continued in use until just after the Second World War. The roof was removed in the 1950s and since 1978 the church has been the responsibility of Harborough District Council. It is believed that Harborough had stronger links to St Mary in Arden chapel than any church in Great Bowden.

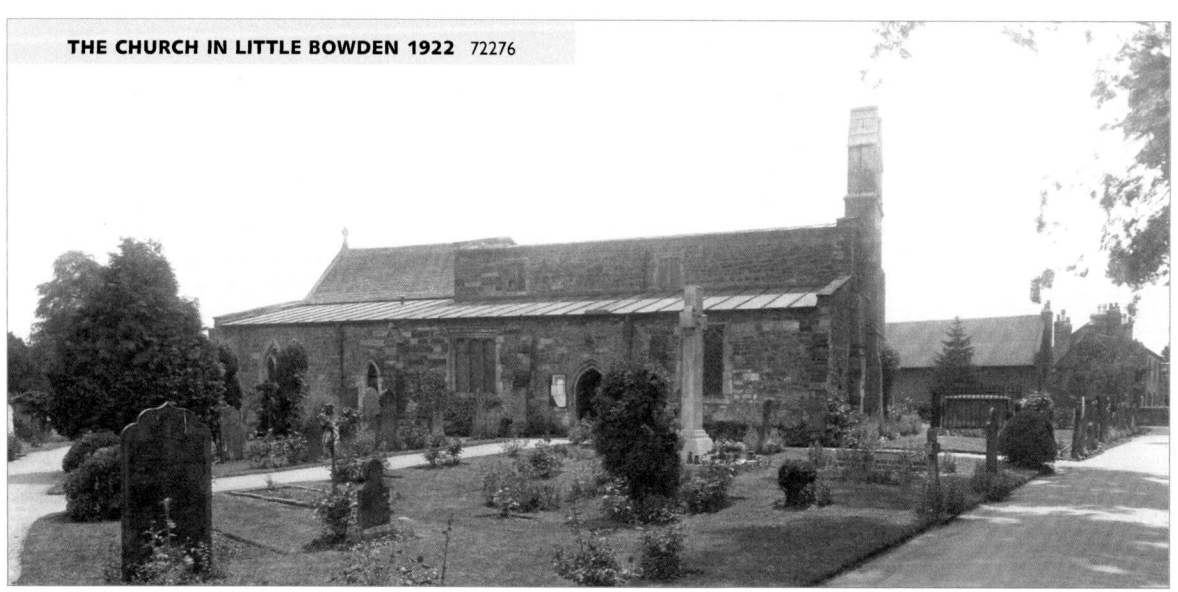

THE CHURCH IN LITTLE BOWDEN 1922 72276

Little Bowden is another one of the hamlets that eventually came to make up Harborough.

Did you know?
Agnes Bowker

Legend has it that in the 1500s a young Harborough woman Agnes Bowker gave birth to a cat. According to official records, the woman claims to have been raped by a cat in the doorway of St Mary in Arden Church. Explanations could be that there was some confusion during the birth and the offspring may have been switched.

Did you know?
Clandestine Marriages

Clandestine marriages were held at St Mary in Arden Church. Harborians were supposed to get married at St Dionysius Church, but preferred St Mary in Arden, even though it was not licensed, because marriages cost much less there. They would still be valid as long as they were performed by a licensed clergyman.

St Marys Road

This road gets its name because it leads up to St Mary in Arden Church, in the village of Arden. In the 18th century it was named St Mary's Lane. As a causeway built over marshland, it was raised to prevent flooding. The photo shows the old post office and the wines and spirit shop, Eady and Dully. The firm had a brewery in Northampton Rd, which closed in 1900 and was demolished in 1908. The site became the bus station in 1960. It is now the Market Hall Car Park. On the left we can see the familiar facade of the National Provincial Bank, now the National Westminster Bank. In the middle distance you can see the Oriental Cinema, which opened in 1921.

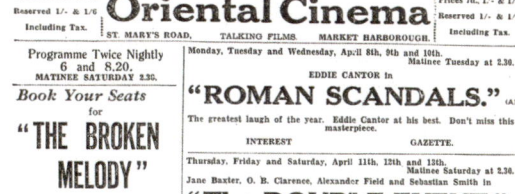

**ADVERTISEMENT FOR
THE ORIENTAL CINEMA** ZZZ01034

ST MARY'S ROAD 1955 M33009

As Harborough grew it swallowed up the village of Little Bowden and Great Bowden became a dormitory suburb. The town was slowly becoming more important than the very villages out of which it had grown. This may have been because of its location close to a crossroads. Two increasingly popular roads crossed at the Three Swans. One route went east to west from Lubenham to Great Bowden; the other went north to south from Leicester to Northampton, via Kibworth and Harborough. The latter of these routes had gardually replaced an old route that had darted from village to village, via Husbands Bosworth and Welford.

Travellers were increasingly attracted to the new route as Harborough developed, and a bitter rivalry formed between the two routes. In 1797 tollhouse keepers on the Harborough Road complained furiously when innkeepers in Husbands Bosworth had diverted traffic onto the Welford Road. The very first building in Harborough was probably situated along this new Harborough route, perhaps where the police station is today, and would have served travellers passing through the town.

Economic development of Harborough may be linked to the aristocracy. During the 12th century, the pursuit of wealth was of paramount concern amongst the upper class, with powerful barons looking for new ways to prosper. Landowners were also constantly looking for ways to increase profit and would embrace any trade or manufacture which seemed lucrative, with varying degrees of success. Barons also saw the moneymaking potential in small market towns that attracted trade and traders from afar. One family - the powerful Mauduits - saw this potential in Market Harborough and are believed to be the first to capitalise on it.

The Mauduits had their domain mainly in the

A KNIGHT AND HIS LADY F6018

Northamptonshire and Buckinghamshire areas of England. William Mauduit II was one of the royal chamberlains whose success had pleased King Henry I so, in 1153, Mauduit was granted the royal estate of Bowden, along with a small hamlet called Market Harborough. It is possible he began developing Harborough as a centre for trade. The Mauduits may also have been politically motivated to develop Harborough because, in doing so, they also created a whole new community that owed everything to the family. It seems they promoted Harborough to a greater extent than the much older centre of Bowden. William Mauduit III succeeded his father in 1158 and was given confirmation of his estates from King Henry II. However, in 1174, William forfeited the land due to his involvement in a revolt against the king. The Mauduits were only in the Bowden area for about 20 years, but they had a major impact on the history of the area, so you could say that it was in the late 12th century, that Market Harborough was born.

Tofts and Yards

Tofts were long, narrow plots of land laid out on both sides of the town street and first came into existence during the Mauduits dominion. Each householder's toft fronted the street with 'yards' behind for workshops, stables or farm buildings. They were originally about 20 yards wide and up to 100 yards long. Attached to the toft would often be a croft, which was a small enclosure for livestock. The tofts have since been divided and built on and many later degenerated to become slum housing for the poor. Examples of tofts still exist at Quakers Yard, Sulleys Yard, Aldwinckles Yard, Millers Yard, Peales Yard, where the Mistrys and MacKays shops are today, and Elands Yard where the town's newspaper was printed for many years. The terms toft and croft are still often used today.

ALDWINCKLES YARD ZZZ01053
This modern photo shows a Harborough yard behind Church Street. The yards became run-down but have since been redeveloped into attractive houses.

Poll tax returns of the late 1300s show a population in Harborough of about 1,000 people. However, outbreaks of the Plague in the town on several occasions resulted in a number of fluctuations in population throughout the Middle Ages. That notorious disease, spread by rats, wiped out a third of the country's population and took many lives in Market Harborough.

According to records, there were attempts to alleviate the symptoms using such diverse ingredients as brandy, cinnamon, frankincense, pepper, saffron and figs, but with little success. Despite the catastrophic effects of the disease when it hit, Harborough's population continued to grow throughout the Middle Ages due, in part, to improvements in medicine. With a healthy population, in more ways than one, and a flourishing market, the town prospered.

Evidence of this prosperity can still be seen today in the shape of the striking St Dionysius Church. Built by the town between 1300 and 1330, the relatively modest church building was offset by a magnificent spire towering 47 metres above the High Street. The broach spire remains one of the finest examples of its kind in England.

PARISH CHURCH 1922 72268

The font replaced a 14th century one which now stands at St Mary in Arden Church.

Originally built as a chapel, St Dionysius' Church was built to celebrate Harborough's growing prosperity. It was dedicated, rather unusually, to St Dionysius, who was the Bishop of Paris in AD240. The dedication of the Harborough chapel to him was probably due to Robert Grosseteste, the Bishop of Lincoln, who was responsible for the Harborough diocese and had great interest in the writings of St Dionysius. The spire was crafted from grey ashlar, while the church itself is ironstone. The chancel axis actually leans slightly, proof that medieval builders had got their measurements wrong.

The interior of the church is quite plain, but it does have some interesting features. The beautiful stained glass window was inserted into the east window in 1860 by the important Birmingham stained glassmaker, John Hardman and depicts the life of Christ in a series of vivid scenes. The chancel's stained glass windows are among the best in Leicestershire.

The church boasted intriguing medieval roof carvings, which could been seen in more detail when the roof was taken down in 1953. Some of the carvings, which adorned huge beams inside the church, had to be burned on account of the ravages of deathwatch beetle, but some can still be seen in the town museum. Although the church has been subject to a number of restorations, it is the only building in Harborough surviving from the medieval period and is inspected every five years. Recently, worrying new cracks have been discovered. The damage, possibly exacerbated by heavy lorries hitting a nearby speed bump, could cost thousands of pounds to repair. It is undeniable, however, that the centre of town radiates from St Dionysius Church, just as it must have done all those centuries ago.

Interestingly, up until 1844, parishioners did not use the main west entrance because the town's fire engine was housed at the bottom of the tower.

THE CHURCH 1965 M33054

The old pulpit was given as a gift to the church from the eight sons of Sir Henry Johnson, Baronet, for the safe return of four of them from an Indian mutiny. It was replaced in 1975 with a wooden pulpit.

ST DIONYIUS' STAINED GLASS ZZZ01052

A closer view of the window's striking colours.

CARVING ZZZ01050

This intricate carving on the north side of the church is probably the head of a bishop.

SUNDIAL ZZZ01051

The sundial on the south face of St Dionysius Church tower dates from about 1762. Taken on a very sunny day in Harborough, this photo captures it casting a definite shadow to show that it is one o'clock. The church's first clock was installed in about 1726 and its present clock appeared in 1902.

Despite its stunning new chapel, during the Middle Ages Harborough was still very much a little brother to the wealthy and more populated Great Bowden. But Harborough would soon begin to assert itself. During the 17th century, growth spurts resulted in the trading community of Market Harborough showing dramatic signs of overtaking the agricultural community of Great Bowden, and soon Harborough would begin to dominate the district. Accentuating the town's growing importance at this time was the building of the Old Grammar School in 1614. Built on posts 'to keep people dry in times of foul weather' and to allow the butter market to continue to be held on the ground floor, it is still one of Market Harborough's best-known landmarks and is still a favourite with postcard producers.

The Old Grammar School was founded by Robert Smyth, Harborough's very own answer to Dick Whittington. He was a poor boy who left Harborough for London 'with

Did you know?
St Dionysius' Church

St Dionysius' Church is one of just a handful of churches in the country that do not have a graveyard. This is because the town is not an ancient settlement but one created out of the parish of Great Bowden where a dependent chapelry at St Mary in Arden already existed. The two chapels were united in 1613 but Harborough residents continued to be buried in the St Mary's graveyard until 1877 when the Northampton Road cemetery opened.

Robert Smyth and the Old Grammar School

THE OLD GRAMMAR SCHOOL 1922 72269p

A group of young children pose for a photograph underneath the Old Grammar School. In the background is the 1889 extension of the Symington's factory which is now the Harborough District Council offices, library and museum.

THE OLD GRAMMAR SCHOOL

1955 M33021

You can just see part of John Briton's The People's Shoe Shop on the right. This attractive stone and iron fronted shop used to house Remingtons, a tailor and breeches maker, who celebrated 100 years in business in 1930.

THE OLD GRAMMAR SCHOOL 1955 M33030

his cup empty' to seek his fortune and found work as an archivist for the Lord Mayor's Court. There he gained an understanding of Latin, the language used in most legal documents at the time and became very successful, but he always remembered the place where he was 'bred and fed' and wanted to do something good with his life.

In order to establish the word of God in the hearts of the people of Harborough, Smyth would often send money up from London to provide bread for the 'godly honest poor' of the town and which would be handed out on the Sabbath day. But he is remembered today for founding the schoolhouse in the Market Place.

The Old Grammar School was in use until 1909 and has, in its time, been given two major restorations, one in 1869 and another in 1977, the latter costing £30,000. A new building was erected for the school in 1892 and in 1910 a third building was built in Burnmill Road. The school is now called Robert Smyth School, after its founder, and boasts 1,500 pupils. The Old Grammar School was fully restored in 1977 and now hosts public events. It has pride of place in Harborough's heritage, reminding us all of an historical age we can only imagine.

Robert Smyth School

The style of the building, designed by Coales and Johnson, is influenced by the work of Christopher Wren. The first head teacher at the Burnmill Road school was Francis Hammond who lived in a house next door. He planted an arboretum on 2.4 acres of land and filled it with many exotic species of plant. He also planted the cedar tree in front of the school. Horticulturalists still enjoy the arboretum today.

BURNMILL ROAD 1960 M33041
Burnmill Road where the Robert Smyth School is today.

THE GRAMMAR SCHOOL, BURNMILL HILL 1955 M33022
This is now the Robert Smyth School.

Did you know?
Intrepid Anthony Jenkinson

Anthony Jenkinson, a pupil of the Old Grammar School in the 16th century Jenkinson had been a merchant, trading mainly in cloth, who travelled the high seas in search of such places as Russia, where he impressed the Tsar, Ivan the Terrible. He logged important information, useful to fellow merchants, about the distance between towns and the time taken to travel between them. But his journeys were full of danger, mainly from bandits. He eventually returned to England and ran diplomatic missions for Queen Elizabeth I and was later charged with the rather unenviable task of ridding the North Sea of pirates, to which purpose he was given a hundred-gun ship.

THE CHURCH AND THE SCHOOL 1960 M33032

How magnificent the church and old school look next to each other.

**THE CHURCH AND SCHOOL
1922** 72266

Even a small dog has stopped in the road to gaze at the view. There is an impressive gas lamp on the right and it is just possible to see a horse and cart delivering goods to local shops on the left.

THE CHURCH AND SCHOOL 1965 M33098

This rear view angle of the old school and church is a vivid reminder of the days before the church square was pedestrianised. Vehicles driving this close to such old buildings must have had a terrible effect on their structures. In 1963, improvements to the church square saw the Old Grammar School and Parish Church set together on an island site with one-way traffic around it. The site was paved in a chequered fashion, benches were introduced and trees were planted. The design was wholeheartedly accepted and led to a Civic Trust Award.

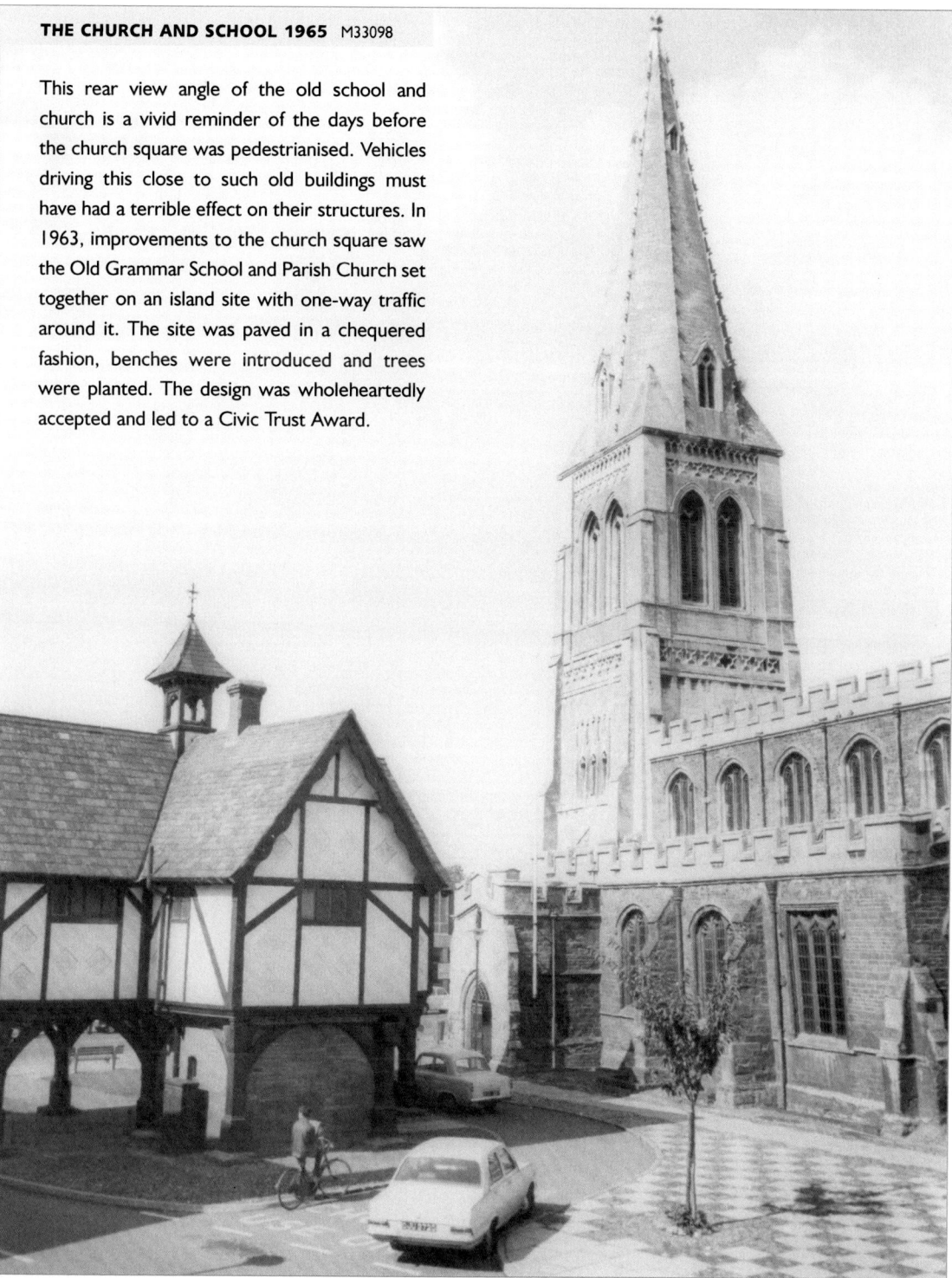

There is one night particularly that changed Market Harborough forever, not to mention the course of British history. On 14 June 1645 the crucial Battle of Naseby was fought just south of Harborough. The battle was to become one of the turning points in the English Civil War.

While waiting for news of the siege by the New Model Army on Oxford, the King made his way through Harborough after a brief stay at Lubenham Hall, on his way to join more of his forces up north. But the cunning parliamentary general Sir Thomas Fairfax sent troops to catch up with the Royalist stragglers and a skirmish ensued at Naseby, in which the Roundheads were victorious. When news of the defeat reached the King, he rode to the King's Head Inn in Harborough for a council of war with his commander and nephew Prince Rupert. They had two options: either they could make a tactical retreat or they could turn and fight. The King chose to fight.

He assembled his army in Harborough and marched them up to high ground between Great Oxendon and Sibbertoft. Here the two armies came face to face. Prince Rupert, however, made an error of judgement by attacking the Roundheads while leaving the core of the King's army exposed. Oliver Cromwell moved in to exploit the weakness and took control of the battle. The Royalists panicked and attempted to flee. The king followed. But many were slaughtered by the Roundheads or captured and imprisoned in St Dionysius Church, one of the town's most secure buildings. That night Oliver Cromwell wrote a letter from The Bell Inn (now in Northampton Road) to Speaker Lenthall in Parliament announcing the parliamentary forces' victory. The king lost the throne and was imprisoned at Holdenby House before being executed by the parliamentary victors. The town's links to the Civil War are evident today with many street names dedicated to the infamous battle: Cromwell, Rupert, Fairfax, Astley, Ireton, Langdale, Skippon, Lenthall, Naseby, Stuart, Montrose and Essex.

After the civil war there was a major change in the appearance of Harborough. Because Harborians began to prosper, their houses became bigger and more ostentatious. Attractive timber and whitewash style buildings were dominant in the 17th century, but there was a new type of building too, the stone house, impressive to look at and a symbol of increasing prosperity throughout the district.

As the Midland Forest was no longer in existence there was little timber available. Thus, the whitewash style buildings, of which the Old Grammar School is our only remaining example, began to disappear. Then the stone house became less common too, and the Peacock in St Mary's Road is now the only surviving stone house from this period. In their place less attractive red brick houses began to appear.

THE PEACOCK 1965 M33056

The picturesque Peacock Hotel is the only surviving stone house in Market Harborough. It was a popular stop for people passing through Harborough in coaches and continues to serve regulars today. The Cock Inn opposite, serving ales and stout, no longer exists. St Mary's Place is now pedestrianised.

The town of Harborough was heavily re-built in the 18th century, a sign of the town's prosperity. Much of the building in the centre of town now dates from this time with the least spoilt examples in the upper High Street.

This is possibly a very similar view to that which stagecoach drivers would have had as they rode into town. On the right you can see the Angel Hotel and J and E Flint, wine and spirit merchants.

UPPER HIGH STREET 1922 72262

LEICESTER ROAD 1922 72270

Entering the town from Leicester Road.

Entering the town today, particularly from Leicester Road, is like entering a town magically caught in yesteryear. It's as if the town has grasped firmly hold of its history and refused to let it go. You can almost imagine riding into the town on a stagecoach as many people would have done during the 1700s. Dozens of coaches would have passed through Harborough every day, bringing trade with them. At the sounding of the guard's horn, passenger coaches thundered off down the High Street destined for London. But they were not without danger, particularly if a horse decided to bolt up the high street! The coaches had exciting names - Telegraph, Courier, Greyhound and Defiance - all giving the impression of speed. Alas, it took up to four days for the heavy cumbersome wagons to reach the capital. The journey time was reduced to two days, 'if God permitted', by gradual improvements to the condition of the roads for which travellers paid a toll at the turnpike gates.

It is thought that Harborough set up one of the country's first turnpikes, with the revenue from them being used to maintain the roads. It followed that as roads improved, the number of travellers passing through Harborough increased, thus furthering the prosperity of innkeepers. In fact, at the end of the 18th century, innkeepers were the largest single group of tradesmen in Harborough. In those days, riding horseback or taking a stagecoach were the most popular means of transport.

COACHING YEARS ZZZ01060

The town's prime location between Northampton and Leicester was probably one of the reasons that it became a major coaching stop. Besides lying as it does on the important London to Manchester route, one of the longest in England, it became a natural place for coach drivers to stop and eat, quench their thirst or change horses. The plethora of inns and taverns that emerged were an essential part of the business and are a sign of the town's importance at the time. They were the motorway service stations of their time.

On your journey through Harborough you would no doubt have stopped off at one of the town's many coaching inns which had grown up on the back of a flourishing market.

LEICESTER ROAD 1922 72271

In the early days of the town, stage coaches would have made their way along this stretch of road, possibly on their way back from Manchester, and stopped at one of Harborough's many inns. Folly Pond is up on the left of the photo, just beyond the two children in shade of the tree.

THE THREE SWANS 1965 M33043p

The Three Swans Hotel is one of the highlights of the High Street. Its eccentric former landlord John Fothergill (1876-1957) wrote memoirs of his experiences running the hotel.

MIDDLE HIGH STREET 1955 M33011p

The Three Swans sign is visible on the left, the Red Cow is on the right and the Town Hall in the centre.

The Three Swans

The Three Swans, formerly known as the Swan, was first mentioned in 1517 and changed its name in about 1790. The hotel even has royal connections. Prince Charles was once brought to the hotel following a hunting accident and, 300 years earlier, on 13 June 1645, King Charles I took refreshment there the day before the Battle of Naseby.

The eye-catching decorative sign - one of the largest and most famous in the country - is made from 18th century wrought iron. It was given a fresh lick of paint in 2003 by local artist Frank Scott.

THE THREE SWANS

AN A.A. & R.A.C. ROSETTE HOTEL

MARKET HARBOROUGH
1517

FOR RESERVATIONS TELEPHONE:
MARKET HARBOROUGH
3247/8 and 2198

ADVERTISEMENT FOR THE THREE SWANS
ZZZ01033

Did you know?
Inns

Inns that sprang up to capitalise on the coaching trade were the Three Swans, Angel, Peacock, Bell, George, Hind, Cock Inn, Old Crown, Green Dragon, Dolphin, King's Head, Talbot and Duke of Wellington. Smaller establishments such as the Red Cow, Cherry Tree, Greyhound, Nag's Head and Freemason's Arms (now the Village Inn) also appeared. The Duke of Wellington is now the Trades and Labour Club in Upper High Street, also known as the Top or Red Club. Its function room is aptly named the Wellington Suite. At the peak of the coaching trade there may have been 50 pubs in town - that's one hell of a pub-crawl!

The street plan of Harborough has changed very little in 800 years In the museum, there is a layout of the town, dating from 1776, which shows a block of shops between Church Street and High Street and some between Factory Lane and the Square. These shops were once temporary market stalls that slowly became permanent houses and shops. It is this town layout - with its main street, parish church, grammar school, two short streets and four lanes off the town centre - that formed the beginnings of Market Harborough as it is today. If the coaching trade was a major factor in shaping Harborough, the town's other economic strength, which would continue to exert its influence, was its weekly market.

CHAPTER TWO

A Market Town

THE MARKET ZZZ01071

IN 2004 Market Harborough celebrates 800 years since its first market. Its influence on the town's history cannot be underestimated and it also explains a lot about the town today. Lying on a crossroads, where the road from Northampton to Leicester crossed the River Welland, the town gradually became a focal point for through trade. But it was in the early 13th century that it truly earned its name when permission to hold a market in Harborough was obtained from the King. It is likely, though, that an unofficial market had been up and running for some time before.

The first mention of a weekly market in Harborough is in the Pipe Roll for the fifth year of the reign of King John (1203). The Pipe Roll was a record of payments and taxes to the exchequer. In the list of new payments in that year is one that translates as: 'The vill of Harborough renders account of three marks for the market. In the treasury (paid) one mark. And it owes two marks'. The total fee of three marks was the equivalent in today's money to £2. In the following year, 1204, Harborough paid a further 10s for the market and later it paid 16s 8d and so paid off its debt. Thus Harborough's weekly market was born.

The infant market flourished, but in 1219 a rival market was set up in neighbouring Rothwell. The Rothwell market traded on the same day (a Monday), which badly affected business on the Harborough market. This move so infuriated the king, he intervened by writing to the Sheriff of Northamptonshire to express his displeasure. The king explained that a new market had been set up 'to the detriment of Harborough's'. His letter, written in Latin, talked proudly of 'mercati nostri' - 'our market'. Nothing happened. Just after Christmas in 1221, the king wrote to the wealthy peasant who held Bowden, giving orders to change Harborough's market to a Tuesday. And so, until the new millennium, the market was held on a Tuesday, but recently market day was changed to a Wednesday so as not to clash with Leicestershire's other remaining livestock market in Melton Mowbray.

With the success of the market at its heart, the town's population grew and continued to prosper. Up until as late as the 1950s, virtually every family that lived in Market Harborough was connected to the market in some way.

It was held in the centre of town, in the High Street and Square, until the 20th century.

The cattle market used to gather in the upper High Street, near to where the Angel Hotel is today, and the sheep market would take over the Square. Horses would be sold on market day on land off Fairfield Road, where Harborough Cricket Ground is now and, in the same street, on the site of the current police station, was the pig market.

Much of the livestock bought at the market would be sold for meat, often to butchers' shops just yards away, but sometimes the animals would end up further afield.

Livestock would be reared just a few miles away in the lush Welland Valley pastures that boasted some of the finest grazing land in the country. Unfattened store cattle would be bought at the market in early spring and fattened in Welland Valley fields before being sold for meat in the autumn and early winter. On market day, the beasts would be led into town by their hundreds.

CATTLE HEADING FOR MARKET ZZZ01069

MARKET 1903 ZZZ01070

THE MARKET c1890-1900 ZZZ01038 (Reproduced by courtesy of Harborough Museum and Andrew Carpenter)

The Square filled with cattle and sheep on market day. It would have been a hive of activity and noise.

In the 1300s, butchers' stalls stood where the Old Town Hall is now and when the Earl of Harborough built the town hall in 1788 the ground floor continued to be reserved for butchers. There were about a dozen butchers in the town during the 1900s and at least two in all the surrounding villages, often dependent on the market for their meat.

The market was also a good source of meat for the Yorkshire pie industry and some of the larger cows would often end up as pie fillings. Meat would also go to the Army.

Did you know?
Frozen Assets

H H Pickering was the first butcher in Market Harborough to install a refrigerator. In fact, it was such a big occasion that, when it was fitted, all the butchers in town visited the shop just to gaze at it. The walk-in fridge was installed in a room that had previously been used as a bank manager's office. It probably wasn't the first time people had walked into that room and been given a frosty reception!

Herbert Halford Pickering

One of the most important butchers in Market Harborough during the early 1900s was Herbert Halford Pickering (1884-1960). His butcher shop had more customers than any other and became famous for its sausages, which used a recipe inherited from a previous town butcher, Holt. H H Pickering started out in the former Holt premises in the High Street, next door to where Chinatown is today. It later moved to premises just over the road, now demolished, where Mistry's chemist business is now.

H H Pickering provided meat for restaurants such as the Angel and pork for Emersons in Northampton Road, to make their pork pies. Mr Pickering, like most butchers, would rely on Harborough's livestock market for his meat. But during the cold winter months the rich pasture land around the town declined in quality, so he would travel to the warmer east coast to buy cattle. After driving to Norfolk and buying about eight steers, he would load the beasts onto a railway wagon, drive back to Harborough and wait for them to arrive. Two he would keep for his own shop; the rest he sold to neighbouring butchers, who relied on him for their meat.

Mr Pickering was chairman of the War Agricultural Committee (Market Harborough District) - a statutory body that implemented Government agricultural policy - and he was also chairman of the Butchers' Association that allocated meat during wartime. In 1945, he received an OBE from the Queen for his services to agriculture.

For many years he was chairman of Market Harborough Urban District Council.

TELEPHONE No. : 2028

H. H. PICKERING
FAMILY BUTCHER

Home-Made Sausages a Speciality

Your Esteemed Orders Solicited

High St., MARKET HARBORO'
(Next to the Midland Bank Limited)

ADVERTISEMENT FOR H H PICKERING ZZZ01032

George Pickering, son of H.H Pickering (see above), who still lives in the town, recalls how, as a boy, he would help walk the cattle into town for market day from Great Oxendon. Other cattle came into town from places as far afield as Medbourne, Welford, Arthingworth, Kelmarsh and Cranoe. 'There were no health and safety regulations', George recalls. 'When I was about five years old we would have to walk cattle up the road. There would often be about 300 beasts walking up the High Street towards the market. It was hardest trying to walk three at a time because, in small groups, you had terrible trouble getting them to walk in the right direction! Sometimes they would wander off and cause road accidents. I remember when a truck ended up in a ditch because of a stray bullock.'

The council had been successful in improving town conditions further by building three new slaughterhouses on

Did you know?

October Fair

One important date in Market Harborough's calendar was the annual October Fair, held in the High Street, which attracted trade from much further afield. The event, dating back to the first ever market, was famous in the East Midlands and would fill the town's streets for about ten days. It was an extremely important occasion for buyers and sellers of horses and other livestock and the streets would come alive with the sounds of traders selling livestock to the highest bidder.

The sights, sounds and smells of market day would whip the town into a weekly frenzy as traders haggled and children watched on with youthful fascination. One of those children was Cedric Ashton, now in his 80s, who remembers the market well as he has lived his whole life in Springfield Street in Harborough, home of the livestock market during the 1900s. He recalls: it was 'like the Wild West with cattle coming at you from all directions. The hustle and bustle of market day was incredible. It was so vibrant, unlike anything you'd see in the town today. I remember my mother angrily shouting at farmers who were leading their cattle up the side alley of our house and leaving trails of mud everywhere'.

He also describes how one of the characters of the market, Jack Sumpter, would wander around carrying a yoke (a wooden frame which fits over the shoulders) with two empty buckets. ' No-one quite knew why he did it, he just did!', said Mr Ashton. He also recalls one market superintendent, Mr Adcock, who ruled the market with a rod of iron, ensuring there was no mess left behind and that no animals were mistreated.

land close to the market. They were rented to butchers in the hope the unsuitable slaughterhouses in the centre of town could be closed. All butchers would do their own killing, mainly at the council-owned slaughterhouse in Springfield Street, near to where the Marand Motors garage is now. Later, when the council slaughterhouse closed, a large, commercial slaughterhouse was built close by, near to where the Ford Sandicliffe garage stands now. A lack of official regulations meant farmers, who had no experience of butchering, would often kill lambs themselves instead of paying for them to be killed at the slaughterhouse. They would then sell the meat around local villages to make money when times were hard between the wars.

As soon as the cattle were sold they were either moved to a small field near the market called a lairage or they were led up towards Great Bowden Road, ready to be loaded on to trains. In later years, of course, the lorry took over the job of the train. Keeping a watchful eye over proceedings was the market superintendent who lived in the Market Lodge, situated where the Sainsbury's petrol station is today.

Cattle Posts

These posts were used, with varying degrees of success, to keep the ungainly animals away from property, shop fronts and businesses on market day when chains would be hung between posts. They can still be seen around Harborough today - between the Old Town Hall and the Red Cow pub, opposite the Parish Church, outside the Angel Hotel and by the Copperfield Hotel on the corner of Welland Park Road. In fact, unusually, some of these posts are listed, in the same way old buildings are, and cannot be removed or tampered with without planning permission.

POSTS ZZZ01049

THE SQUARE 1922 72263

The sheep market was held in The Square up until 1903. You can still see the Brooke Memorial Fountain, built in 1890, in memory of Sir William De Capell Brooke of Brooke House in recognition of his philanthropy. Both animals and people used the fountain for drinking. It was later moved to a new home near the parish church.

Note the old-fashioned clothes of the children on the left

THE MARKET PLACE 1922 72264t

MIDDLE HIGH STREET c1965 M33039p

This photo of a busy day in the town centre, although taken after the market moved, gives some idea of the chaos that there must have been when shopkeepers tried to run their businesses with hundreds of cows, pigs and sheep ambling down the High Street. You can see the Brooke Memorial Fountain in its new home outside the parish church (it was later removed as it became a traffic hazard). On the left are Crockatts dry cleaners and Liptons, a multiple retailer in the grocery trade specialising in tea. Note the shimmering star above the Talbot sign. The archway next to the pub, obscured by Lipton's canopy, would have given access to stabling for horses in the days of stagecoaches. You can also see Mawer and Saunder's, ironmongers and hardware store.

During the early years, on market days, pedestrians were always in danger of being trampled by the large, unpredictable beasts as traders attempted to line them up for viewing. The High Street market also caused major disruption to daily commercial life and posed a considerable health problem. Dung heaps, which covered the streets after the market was cleared away, created an unsightly and unwanted mess in the pretty town centre. Piles of dung would have probably been swept into an open storm drain, the town dike, which would have run down the High Street from Folly Pond in Leicester Road, under the Square and finally out into the River Welland. There are written records of repair work to a number of bridges that ran over this small dike. They are no longer in existence. Later this drain was confined to an artificial channel, and the water from Folly Pond controlled for use in fighting fires. Eventually it was enclosed in a culvert and covered over, allowing much more room for through traffic.

Inevitably, given the disruption they caused, the markets were not popular with everyone. More than 2000 beasts roaming the streets created a substantial nuisance.

In 1903 the council decided to move the livestock market to a purpose built site off Springfield Street, where the Sainsbury's car park is today. The move was controversial: before making its decision, the council had held a town poll to gauge public opinion - something that rarely happens today - 858 people voted in favour of moving the market and 739 voted against it. It was a close thing, but the council could go ahead and bought the Market Rights from the lord of the manor for nearly £2,500, and twelve acres of land. H Winter Johnson designed a model cattle market, with six acres laid out for the market and the remaining six for open lairages for stock bought on site. The new market was born.

This move, in effect, swept the market from the streets and paved the way for a number of town improvements. In 1938, during a major

THE SETTLING ROOMS ZZZ01048

The Grade II listed Settling Rooms, designed by H G Coales and H W Johnson, is all that remains of the original market. The building, now surrounded by Sainsbury's car park, was used for settling up after the auctioneer had completed the selling of livestock. It is now used by the Volunteer Bureau and Council for Voluntary Services, with a cafe and exhibition area.

overhaul of town centre, the chairman of the council officially opened the semi-covered General Market, later replaced by the Market Hall. After some initial quibbling, stall holders agreed to move their pitches from the Square to the General Market, which complemented the Springfield Street livestock market and traded weekly for most of the 20th century.

Traditionally on market day the farmers would attend to business on the livestock market, while their wives would get the weekly shopping at the general market.

Post-war changes brought about a gradual decline in Harborough's livestock market. After the Second World War the new trend was towards growing cereals. The Government put pressure on farmers to grow grain instead of keeping livestock and farmers were urged to plough their land instead of keeping cattle on it. They were of the opinion that the rich Welland Valley pastureland was too good to plough and many farmers protested at the imposed changes. Despite the decline, the market continued in Harborough up until 1993 when, after much discussion, the Springfield Street market closed and moved to the site of an old army camp between Lubenham and Foxton. This controversial move ended the livestock market's links with Harborough dating back almost 800 years.

THE MARKET HALL ZZZ01047

The Market Hall opened in 1993 and replaced the old General Market. It is filled with stalls three days a week and on its roof is a six-foot high weather vane depicting the spire of St Dionysius and the Old Grammar School. Next to it there is now a car park where there was once a brewery and, later, a bus station.

MARKET SCULPTURE ZZZ01046

This wonderful brick sculpture, found in St Mary's Place, often goes unnoticed by the scores of people who walk by it, but it remains a visual reminder of the town's once thriving livestock market.

THE MARKET TODAY ZZZ01045 (Photo by Andrew Carpenter)

The market today, now situated on an old army camp in Lubenham.

VICTORIAN COUNTY MAP OF LEICESTERSHIRE FEATURING MARKET HARBOROUGH c1850

CHAPTER THREE

Industrialisation

AS IN the rest of the country, the Victorian age was an era of dramatic change for Market Harborough: the arrival of the railway, the canal and beginnings of major industry would have far-reaching effects and would change the town forever. It was a time of transformation and rapid expansion and the town made the most of the industrial revolution with many in business who achieved great success. But with prosperity came poverty.

The first great innovation of the 19th century in Harborough was the canal. There had been much debate towards the end of the previous century about the possibilities of extending the Leicester canal, but there were concerns about engineering difficulties. The canal was initially extended to the village of Gumley, just outside Harborough, but this wasn't ideal as traders still had to haul their goods all the way to Gumley. Eventually the canal was carved through the countryside, continuing into Foxton, Great Bowden and finally reaching Market Harborough in 1809. The Harborough Arm of the Grand Union Canal was created.

The original idea had been to develop the Harborough canal to Northampton, but this was considered too costly. Instead, it was decided it should join up with the Grand Union Canal, which went from London to Birmingham. One of the canal's major problems was addressed in 1814 when a famous series of locks was designed to allow

THE CANAL c1965 M33091

boats to climb the 75ft hill at Foxton, up one side of the Welland Valley to Husbands Bosworth. The locks were temporarily replaced at the turn of the 20th century by an experimental inclined plane, a considerable feat of engineering at the time. The lift dramatically reduced the time it took to travel the incline, but did not prove a long-term success. It was not used after 1910 and was dismantled in 1928. There is still evidence of it next to the current locks at Foxton, which remain a hugely popular tourist attraction.

Once it was completed, traders immediately took advantage of the Harborough wharf. Coal and corn were the two most important goods being transported to surrounding areas at this time. Stagecoaches could only carry about five tons and there were complaints about the damage caused to the roads by the heavy loads. The canal boats could carry 20 times that amount, with less horse and manpower. It was clearly the more efficient and economic means of transporting commercial goods.

CANAL BOATHOUSES 1922 72274

In the distance, people carry canoes on to the river outside Foster's Boathouse and Tea Gardens. The bridge in the background carried the A6 and has now been replaced. Harry Foster later turned the boathouse into a motel called Uncle Tom's Night Club.

FOXTON, GRAND UNION CANAL 1960 FI59004p

CANAL BRIDGE 1922 72272p

THE BOATHOUSE 1965 M33090

The boathouse pictured belonged to Hillcrest, the home of keen sportsman Sir Humphrey de Trafford who set up a polo club in Harborough. Hillcrest has since been demolished and is now the site of the Woodlands estate.

THE CANAL c1960 M33054j

As well as providing Harborough with an important transport facility, the canal provided a stretch of water for sport and pleasure. Rowing boats could be hired from one of the many boathouses situated along the banks of the canal. Even sailing boats could be spotted drifting along its stretches, complete with a gramophone playing the songs of the time.

There were also Water Carnivals, where narrow boats, some full of children, would fill the basin while hundreds of people lined the canal banks to watch. Today, the wharf at Harborough is one of the most picturesque sights in the town. Surrounded by luxury flats, the wharf remains filled with narrow boats and has that quintessential laid-back atmosphere of the waterways.

HARBOROUGH WHARF TODAY ZZZ01044

THE BOATHOUSE 1965 M33090

Even greater than the impact of the canals was the coming of the railways, which brought with it increased trade and more local success stories. Where the weekly market was once the heart that kept the town alive, the railway arguably overtook the market as the town's economic pulse. It had become the vital tool of industry.

The London and North Western Railway (LNWR) built the first railway through Market Harborough in 1850 as part of its route from Rugby to Stamford. The station yard was on land that would be later occupied by the warehouses of Tungstone Batteries. Seven years later, the Midland Counties Railway opened a line running from Leicester and calling at Harborough, Bedford and Hitchin. This was later extended from Bedford to London St Pancras, giving Harborians a direct train route to the capital. The first trains took just over four hours to get to London - dramatically faster than the stagecoach, which had taken four days to do the same journey! Though relatively slow by today's standards, the railways did revolutionise travel.

At that time there were two independently operated train stations in Harborough, just yards from one another. It was a cutthroat industry and Victorian businessmen, particularly those involved with the railways, were a ruthless breed. There was fierce rivalry between the two Harborough stations as they competed for acquisition of new routes and the custom of more passengers. In 1923 the two stations put their rivalry behind them and merged.

The people who worked on the trains in Harborough were affectionately known as the Loco Men. They were a tough lot and had to be. Trains were steam-powered, relying on engine men to continually shovel coal into the engine. It was incredibly demanding, as the engine man would often have to shovel between three and four tons of coal per journey. This would lead to many arguments between driver and engine man. If the engine man could not keep up the shovelling, the train would slow down and fall behind schedule. Both would then have to face the wrath of the Shed Master or perhaps one of the fearsome Loco Inspectors. With the job came great responsibility, as there was always

Did you know?
Thomas Cook

A Harborough cabinetmaker named Thomas Cook, who had a workshop in Buzzard's Place, organised the first railway excursion. Cook had a deep interest in evangelical work and in 1834, while walking from Harborough to Leicester, he came up with the idea of using the railway to transport a large number of people from Leicester to Loughborough to a religious rally. He succeeded in persuading the railway company that, even at a fare of just 1s a head, it would be profitable. He went on to become world famous as the founder of the travel agents Thomas Cook and Son. He is, undoubtedly, Market Harborough's most famous son.

the danger that a train driver may misread a signal in thick fog, for example, and cause a major crash. The Loco Men of Harborough were often difficult to get to know and would guard their highly respected jobs jealously. If an engine man had proved his worth, he may have been lucky enough to earn a promotion to a freight train driver and from there to passenger train driver - the ultimate prize. It took most Loco Men until they were into their 60s before making it to this level.

The trains were extremely important to Harborough because they put the town back on the main route. Their increased use, however, hit the town's coach house trade badly. Some landlords tried to buck the trend by sending employees to meet passengers at the train station and entice them to sample the hospitality of their inn. Symingtons Corset Factory would send a horse-drawn cart to the train station to meet important clients. This was to become known as a Hansom Cab because it was run by a Mr Hansom, and was kept in the Willow Court yard, which can still be seen in St Mary's Road, near to the fish and chip shop.

Did you know?

Oil Lamp Mistaken for Signal

An oil lamp on the railway bridge in Great Bowden Road was removed at the request of Midland Railway Company in 1886 because their drivers kept mistaking it for a signal.

SYMINGTON'S POSTER ZZZ01025
(Reproduced thanks to Leicestershire County Council Heritage Services, Harborough Museum Collection and the Courtaulds Group).

In 1858 a house was converted into an indoor corn exchange to attract trade and capitalise on the ease of importing goods via the railways. The original corn exchange had been outside the Three Swans in the High Street, where the Golden Wonder offices stand today in Abbey Street.

In 1859, the LNWR opened its line from Harborough to Northampton, a route that no longer exists, much to the disappointment of Harborians who work in Northampton.

It is now a cycle track running from Little Bowden Rec to Chapel Brampton. The main London line is all that exists now.

By the mid-1900s Harborians would begin to use the train to get to London, now a straightforward day trip, to see a West End show or visit the sights of the capital. At the time the station employed more than 200 people, mainly as drivers, engine men, signalmen and technical workers. One can just imagine the struggle they must have had trying to deal with the 1,000 cattle that passed through the station every week from the market to be loaded on to trains. Ironically, in spite of the massive increase in the number of trains that pass through Harborough nowadays, there are less than ten people working there.

HARBOROUGH RAILWAY STATION ZZZ01043

Recently the train station, unusual in its grand and opulent design, won the prestigious Ian Allen National Railway Heritage Award. In 2004, it scooped an award from the Rail Passengers Committee, a statutory watchdog, commending the station's staff, environment and facilities.

The impact of further recent improvements to rail services, particularly in terms of speed and efficiency, can be compared to the dramatic changes that trains made when they first arrived in Harborough, about which there will be more in Chapter 5.

An economic boom led to a demographic boom as industrialists began to establish factories and people from neighbouring villages came into the town to work.

The most enterprising tradesmen in Victorian Harborough were the Symington brothers, William and James. They came from Nithsdale in Scotland (hence the name of the Harborough street). William began as a tea dealer and lived in a house in the High Street. James arrived in Harborough later and they went into partnership in 1841, working from a stay-making (corset) outlet in Church Street.

James Symington was also doing well and moved into a shop in the High Street, now Clinton Cards. His son Robert went to America to seek his fortune and met Isaac Merritt Singer, the inventor of the sewing machine. Impressed, he sent three sewing machines back to Harborough for his mother to use in the stay-making factory, thus becoming one of the first manufacturers in Britain to use sewing machines. With business thriving, Robert and his brother William went on to start a corset factory in the old carpet factory in Factory Lane and Adam and Eve Street, and by 1881 they needed to add a further three storeys above the existing three storeys of the Factory Lane premises. By 1884 their great new factory would dominate the centre of town.

The corset factory went from strength to strength, despite Robert Symington's sudden death in 1892. At the peak of their business the company had branches in Desborough, Welford, Rothwell, Rugby and Leicester and employed more than 1,500 people. In Harborough, the factory had become a major employer. Staff who worked at the factory at the time were often ordered to work in silence and would be fined by the timekeeper if they were ever late for work.

ADVERTISEMENT FOR SYMINGTON'S LIBERTY BODICE
ZZZ01037 (Reproduced thanks to Leicestershire County Council Heritage Services, Harborough Museum Collection and the Courtaulds Group)

Symington's most famous innovation, the Liberty Bodice. It continued to be made until the 1950s.

SYMINGTON'S SWEDISH MAIDENS ZZZ01036
(Reproduced thanks to Leicestershire County Council Heritage Services,
Harborough Museum Collection and the Courtaulds Group)

Symingtons' ladies place stitched corsets on Swedish Maidens, heated female forms, to be shaped before being ironed.

Finished corsets were sold mainly to wholesalers rather than to individual retailers. These wholesalers would then sell on to smaller outfitters such as J Wood and Sons, who did a roaring trade in Symingtons' corsets in the Square in Harborough.

Corsets had to be displayed very tastefully in shop windows in such a way as to only hint at the female body shape. The idea of showing the female form or using a mannequin in a shop window would have caused outrage at the time.

Later, during the Second World War, Symingtons' workers played an important role producing more than one million man-carrying parachutes for the RAF. The name Symingtons suddenly appeared all over the world when branches were opened in such places as Johannesburg in South Africa, Melbourne and Adelaide in Australia, Wellington and Auckland in New Zealand and Hobart in Tasmania. These branches were staffed by Harborians, who were shipped over to run the international factories.

Symingtons' Factory Lane premises, which had stood empty ever since the 1950s, were demolished in 1973. The bell tower was saved and moved to Welland Park. The neighbouring Symingtons factory would later become the offices of Harborough District Council, library, museum and tourist information office. The building remains an attractive feature of the town.

In 1850 William built his first coffee-roasting factory in Northampton Road. He also started to manufacture pea-flour, used in soup making and supplied it in bulk to the Government for troops fighting in the Crimea. In 1881 he took his son Samuel into partnership and they built an impressive new factory in Springfield Street. The famous explorer Captain Scott chose the firm's flour and pea soup as part of his supplies for his antarctic expedition in 1904.

BURNMILL ROAD c1965 M33068

Symington's factory in the distance dominates Harborough's skyline

Did you know?

Another important industrial company in Harborough was The Harboro Rubber Co, begun in 1894 by Arthur Briggs and still in the family under the management of his relation, James Briggs. The factory became known as the Day and Night Mills because its employees worked shifts around the clock making rubber soles, tyres and bicycle pedals. This is the origin of the trade name Dainite, which is also the name of the firm's local football team, although very few Harboro Rubber employees play for them now.

COVER OF HARBORO RUBBER CO ZZZ01061

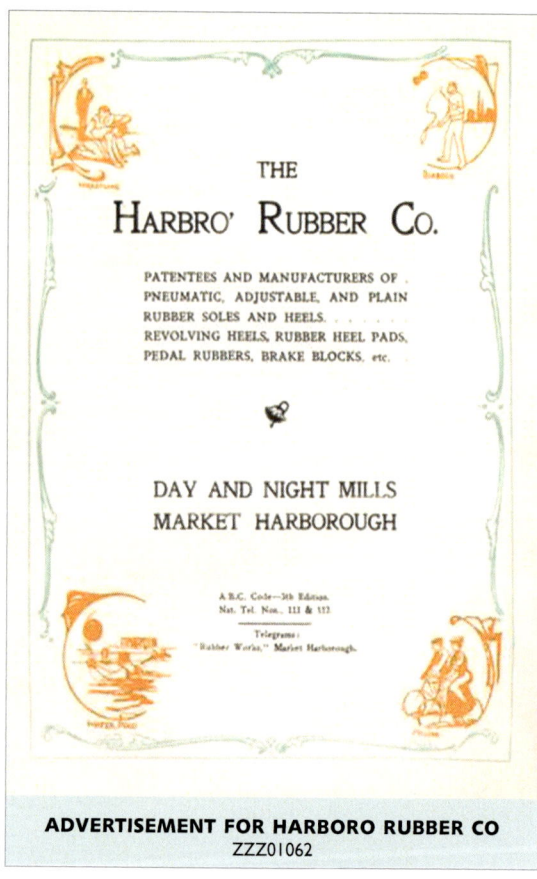

ADVERTISEMENT FOR HARBORO RUBBER CO
ZZZ01062

ADVERTISEMENT FOR HARBORO RUBBER CO ZZZ01035

WORKERS AT HARBORO RUBBER CO ZZZ01039

ADVERTISEMENT FOR

HARBORO RUBBER HEELS ZZZ01063

MARKET HARBORO RUBBER CO FACTORY 1935 ZZZ01027

EXTERIOR VIEW OF THE DAY AND NIGHT MILLS.
MARKET HARBOROUGH.

THE DAY AND NIGHT MILLS ZZZ01064

The works of the Harboro' Rubber Company, in St Mary's Road. Because the factory operated round the clock it became known as the Day and Night Mills.

THE TRIMMING ROOM,

HARBORO RUBBER CO ZZZ01065

repeated, and convinced businesses it was cheaper to advertise in the paper than to use printed bills. The oldest copy of the paper still in existence is dated 2 January 1854, and boasts a 'miscellany of amusing, instructive and entertaining knowledge' beneath its masthead. This claim is somewhat justified by the unusual and, at times, outrageous stories inside. Articles featured included Dr Franklin's 'Code of Morals' and a piece on 'Active Women' which stated: 'As a general rule, noisy women do much less than they seem to do and quiet women often do more'. It went on to claim that 'six out of ten are indolent and only work on compulsion'. Some of the unusual products advertised in its pages were Woodcock's Celebrated Wind Pills and the New Universal Pocket Pencil - with ever-pointed lead the whole length!

In 1890 the Northamptonshire Printing and Publishing Company launched a rival publication, 'The Market Harborough Mail'. In 1923 the two papers merged to become 'The Market Harborough Advertiser and Midland Mail', later to become the 'Harborough Mail', still read today. Unusually, the Thursday publication date of the 'Harborough Mail' does not coincide with a market day in the town, which is untypical of a newspaper. Harborough historians are much indebted to William Eland for establishing a newspaper as it has given them an invaluable record of important events and changes in the town.

Another example is Tungstone, which began in 1898 in Lathkill Street and manufactured in the town for 105 years. Behind every great shopkeeper, there was a great manufacturer and these combined perfectly resulting in a period of growth in the town.

In 1854 local stationer and printer, William Eland, published the town's first newspaper, the 'Market Harborough Advertiser', as a monthly issue. The local news was printed in a cellar in Church Street and the rest of the paper, which featured national news, was bought in pre-printed. Eland seized the opportunity when advertising duty was

The Harborough Mail would move into offices on the right of this picture in 1965. Also on the right is a sign for Emersons, which merged with High Street store Wests, makers of the famous Harborough Cheesecake. Between Monks furniture store, on the right, and the bridge are the workshops for St Mary's Motor Co.

NORTHAMPTON ROAD c1955 M33019p

In the latter part of the 19th century, times were changing and, with companies like Symingtons booming, the town's prosperity led to a demand for new housing. To meet this demand, the Market Harborough Land Society was set up with the intention of selling land for development. The Market Harborough Building Society was also set up to lend money to people who needed it to buy a home. Harborough entrepreneur George Gardiner, who had a street off Coventry Road named after him, was a pivotal member of the Land Society. It was just a small society but hugely influential on the way Market Harborough developed. The society sold small plots of land to people who would then commission a developer to build on it. Developers also built a number of new houses themselves with a view to renting them out to local people. This plot formation is still clear today.

Where there were once just fields stretching from Nelson Street to Lubenham, hundreds of houses began to spring up in streets such as Nelson Street, Hearth Street, East Street, Logan Street, Highfield Street, Spencer Street, Wartnaby Street and Clarke Street. The area of new development came to

THE HARBOROUGH MAIL OFFICES IN NORTHAMPTON ROAD TODAY ZZZ01042

The attractive building was formerly used by the Market Harborough Building Society, which later moved to Welland House on the Square for fear of flooding. Since 2002, there have been several incidents of flooding at the Harborough mail offices.

be known as New Harborough, and is still known by that name 120 years later!

AERIAL VIEW 1935 ZZZ01072

COVENTRY ROAD c1955 M33003

When New Harborough was created many new streets appeared off Coventry Road. The road was widened in the late 19th century at the point where it meets the Square.

Did you know?

Logan Street and Logan Recreation Ground

Liberal MP Paddy Logan, who lived in East Farndon, gave a piece of grassland to the people of New Harborough to beautify the area. He had acquired a lot of land through his job as a railway contractor and instead of building on it, he offered it for use as a recreation ground. Some have said that his gesture was politically motivated, as he may have thought that the land would attract a better class of person to move into the area, one that would vote Liberal rather than Conservative. Logan Street is named after him and the land is now known as the Logan Street Recreation Ground.

In 1901 the Coach and Horses and Ridley's Yard were pulled down to make way for Abbey Street, which provided a route from the High Street to the new area of housing. Then later, the creation of Goward Street extended Abbey Street into New Harborough.

In Nelson Street, until recently, you found the New Harborough Post Office, built originally as a bakery, by George Gardiner. He lived there and his daughter, Annie Gardiner was the first person to be born in the building; at that time most people were born at home. George Gardiner's son-in-law was the successful Harborough butcher Herbert Pickering mentioned in Chapter 2.

The town was expanding in all directions. Until this time there would have been very few houses between the magistrates' court and Great Bowden, between Heygate Street and the bottom of Burnmill hill and beyond Scotland Road heading out towards Northampton. It just shows how times have changed.

NORTHAMPTON ROAD c1955 M33017

Northampton Road was developed from Springfield Street through the 1880s, but most of the roads off Northampton Road didn't appear until the Edwardian period. You can still see the Urban District Council's former offices in Northampton Road. The building was previously the Little Bowden Police Station and courts. It is now used for commercial purposes.

In the old town there had been severe overcrowding. The old yards accommodated half the town's population and the overseers of the poor had a lot of work to do to turn the situation around. A workhouse in Leicester Road was built to provide work for the poor and disabled in exchange for food and shelter. The people came from any one of the 42 parishes that funded the Union, which ran the workhouse. St Luke's Hospital now occupies the site.

The yards of Harborough, in the old town, had become run-down and uninhabitable after repeated extensions had been added. Residents complained incessantly about the disgusting living conditions, the poor drinking water and the lack of a sewerage system.

This unrest led to the creation of the Market Harborough, Great and Little Bowden Urban District, overseen by a Local Board elected by ratepayers, which did what it could to improve sanitation. It eventually got new sewers laid and drinking water piped from wells at Husbands Bosworth. In 1895 the board was replaced by the Market Harborough Urban District Council, a forerunner of the Harborough District Council, which would lead the town into the 20th century.

The situation was also helped by the new housing estates, which dispersed people from the town centre and reduced overcrowding.

YARDS 1933 ZZZ01075

MARKET HARBOROUGH ORDNANCE SURVEY MAP 1899-1902

CHAPTER FOUR

Of War and Reconstruction

RAILWAYS c1955 ZZZ01074

THE LAST 100 years of Market Harborough, its 20th century history if you like, boast some of the town's most colourful, memorable and significant occasions. It was also a century of major town improvements, one of the first of which was clearing the livestock market from the streets. In 1903, the market moved from the High Street and Square to Springfield Street, changing the town centre forever. Its opening was a real occasion for the town and drew people from all over to see the market gates swing open for the first time.

The council built the fire station in 1903 and extended it ten years later with a new wing for the St John Ambulance Brigade. There is evidence of a town fire service run by volunteers, dating back as far as the 1740s when the first fire engine was bought. But there was no organised service until 1870 when local solicitor J L Douglass

became captain of the Volunteer Fire Brigade, later changing its name to the Market Harborough Fire Brigade. The water for fire fighting came from Folly Pond in Leicester Road, which was dug out to create a stream of water through the town and side streets in case of fire. However, in the early 1900s the town acquired a new steam-powered fire engine with a jet hose - tested in dramatic fashion against the steeple of the parish church.

One memorable fire the service was called on to extinguish was in 1905 when an horrific fire swept through the tannery, situated where the Commons Car Park is today. The tannery had probably been there in some form since medieval times. Its prime location close to the river, which was ideal for the industry, would have undoubtedly aided fire fighters at the scene.

FIRE BRIGADE 1904 ZZZ01073

Note the fire chief (left) and his men stood in the remains of the factory.

THE TANNERY AFTER THE FIRE 1905 ZZZ01057

Not everyone would have been sorry to see the tannery go up in flames. The process of tanning, whereby animal hide is converted into leather, produced a by-product of hair and lime, which blocked the sewers. It was also difficult to extract dye from the water system and the tannery also emitted a smell of rotten eggs, caused by sulphuretted hydrogen, the subject of many complaints to the council. But the tannery survived the fire and continued until 1913. Its towering chimneystack, however, was not demolished until 1965.

In 1911 the town was in patriotic mood for King George V's coronation with High Street shops and houses flying flags to mark the occasion and a major celebration on the Square with virtually all the town's children in attendance. But the jubilant mood would not last.

Having started the 1900s welcoming Harborough soldiers back from the Boer War, the people of the town would again experience the harsh realities of conflict before the century was out.

THE TANNERY CHIMNEY BEING DEMOLISHED ZZZ01058

The war periods brought people in Market Harborough together in ways they had never experienced before. A community spirit united the town at times of both grief and celebration.

Over the next couple of years organised meetings were held urging Harborough men to enlist to help the war effort. The cattle market was turned into a depot used for supplying horses to the army. Wooden huts were built to act as stables. There was a war workers depot in Upper High Street, which became the centre for women's voluntary work during the First World War. After the war, returning servicemen received grateful and joyous greetings. A two-day celebration was held and 800 servicemen were given a dinner at the Assembly Rooms which spilled over into Abbey Street due to the lack of space.

The backlog of work after the war was enormous, particularly in terms of housing. Many houses had become unfit for people to live in. They were damp, run-down and cramped, most of them in the yards, and there was an urgent need for new homes. A demolition programme, known as the slum clearance programme, was put in place to rid the town of its unfit houses. A new site off Northampton Road was chosen for council

FIRST TO WAR, 6 AUGUST 1914 ZZZ01059

The Harborough Territorials parading on the Square before marching to Loughborough to meet other Leicestershire companies at the beginning of the First World War. They were the first detachment of Harborough men to go to house development and named Welland Park Road. The first council houses, two rather nice semi-detached premises in the Broadway, were occupied in 1920 and in the ten years after the war 400 houses were built, 164 owned by the council, but the demand for council houses was high and the waiting list growing.

A further 50 new council houses were completed in 1935 and called Walcot Road. This area became run down in the latter part of the 20th century, but recently under- went a major re-building programme that has transformed the street into an attractive part of the town.

The new homes were not always as welcomed as might have been expected. When people from the yards were moved to the newly built Ridgeway they felt they had lost

> ## *Did you know?*
> ### German POW Operates First Combine Harvester
> *It is claimed that the first ever combine harvester was used on a farm in Lubenham, just outside Market Harborough, by a German prisoner of war, an ex-Luftwaffe pilot who came to Harborough as a POW and worked on the farm. After the war, he opted to stay and eventually went on to marry an evacuee and settle in Harborough.*

the community spirit they had experienced living in the yards. But, nevertheless, between the end of the First World War and the start of the Second World War II, more than 1,000 houses were built in Harborough.

WELLAND PARK ROAD c1955 M33014

100 council houses were built in Welland Park Road to relieve poor living conditions in the old yards. These were completed in 1934.

WELLAND PARK HIGH SCHOOL c1955 M33008

In the 1930s, a piece of land was sold to the county council for a new modern school. This became Welland Park High School and later Welland Park Community College, which now teaches both children and adults.

Did you know?
Electricity Arrives

Electricity first arrived in Market Harborough in 1924, and in just three years, half the town was connected. Like everywhere else, electricity revolutionised the town and the way Harborians lived. The Market Harborough Urban District Council had enquired about the possibility of its Kettering equivalent, which had been supplying electricity to its residents since 1904, supplying the town of Harborough. Kettering Urban District Council agreed to supply Harborough, if it could be proved there were enough customers to make it pay. There were enough customers and soon Harborough was plugged into the modern age.

Did you know?
Library

In 1929 the first library in Market Harborough was established in Abbey Street with an initial stock of just over 1,000 books. On its first evening 323 people enrolled. After just two months, more than 6,000 issues had been made. The council employed a librarian for £1 a week and by 1931 had issued 57,000 books. It was later moved to Welland House, and then moved to a house in the Square, formerly used as a private school, and which the owner had willed for use as a library, provided it was used for the 'benefit of the town'.

Welland Park

Welland Park was a welcome addition to the town in the 1930s. There were allocations for a bowling green, tennis courts, golf putting course, a sports ground and in the centre a garden, pavilion, cafe and bandstand.

WELLAND PARK BOWLING GREEN c1955 M33004

WELLAND PARK PUTTING GREEN

c1955 M33028

WELLAND PARK TENNIS COURTS c1955 M33007
These tennis players seem a bit overdressed today!

THE BANDSTAND c1955 M33024
The bandstand, which people danced around on VJ Day, still hosts performances by Harborough Band and its junior band.

WELLAND PARK TENNIS COURTS c1955 M33007

Carnival

In 1931, a tradition began in Harborough that would continue to this day, growing into the biggest and most popular event in the town's social calendar. Harborough Carnival was started that year to raise funds for the cottage hospital in Coventry Road. This still happens today, but with many other charities and organisations benefiting too.

DORIS ROBINSON (NEE GILBERT) AS CARNIVAL QUEEN IN 1931 ZZZ01068

DORIS ROBINSON 2004
ZZZ01066

The carnival queen at that very first event, Doris Gilbert (later Doris Robinson), was chosen after photographs of all the carnival queen contestants were published in the 'Harborough Mail'. Readers then voted for their favourite in exactly the same way the queen is chosen today. Doris (90) who still lives in Harborough, recalls:

'We walked from a house near the Northampton Road bridge to the float, which was beautifully decorated with flowers. A young boy walked in front of me with the crown on a plush red cushion. I was then crowned by Lady Lock-Elliot of Hallaton. It was a lovely experience and a real honour to be the town's first ever carnival queen'.

A good number of floats paraded with the queen's including entrants from the cottage hospital and Tungstone Batteries. Carnival revellers also made good use of Symington's Recreation Ground, which had opened ten years previously and which in later years would become a focal point of carnival day.

Harborough Carnival, begun in 1931, became a joyous annual occasion, but peacetime and the feeling of security that comes with it would soon end. In 1939, the people of Harborough suddenly had less frivolous things on their minds. When the Second World War broke out, people soon realised that it wasn't just the soldiers on the front line who were in danger of losing their lives. There was a real fear in the town about poison gas bombs being dropped in air raids.

Despite this, with rural areas deemed safer than the cities, evacuees arrived at Harborough train station in their droves: in September 1939, 3,250 children, mothers and babies arrived in the town. The evacuees would gather in the Market Hall before being taken to their new homes in the town or neighbouring villages. To add to an already difficult situation, there was an outbreak of scarlet fever amongst the evacuees and an impromptu Fever Hospital was set up in Fairfield Road. Many children were also found to have the skin disease scabies. When the expected bombing of major cities did not happen immediately, many evacuees were sent home. They returned, however, between 3,000 and 4,000 in all, when bombs were dropped on London in September 1940.

Market Harborough escaped bombardment, although air raid drills were carried out in the town just in case. On 8 April 1941, however, five bombs fell on Great Bowden, causing only minor damage and no loss of life.

Did you know?
POW Football Matches

Football matches were organised between the prisoner of war camps in Farndon Road, which held mainly Germans and Italians. The POWs were not allowed to play with the locals. This, however, did not stop the odd German or Italian ringer being drafted in to play for some of the local village teams.

Memorial Cross

The memories of the 248 Harborians who had lost their lives in the First World War were honoured in the town. The dedication of the war memorial, designed by a Wellingborough man, W Talbot Brown and paid for by public subscription, took place on Sunday, 25 September 1921. After the dedication service, wreaths laid by families and friends virtually covered the memorial.

A film of this emotional event was made at the time and can be seen in Harborough Museum.

Plaques inscribed with the names of the dead were added later and surplus money collected for the war memorial paid for the memorial wing of the cottage hospital.

MEMORIAL CROSS 1922 72265

MEMORIAL CROSS 1922   72265

The Gardens

THE GARDENS c1960 M33048

THE GARDENS OF REMEMBRANCE c1965 M33076

The War Memorial Garden of Remembrance in Welland House garden was officially opened in July 1954. A house that had belonged to a Gulliver Speight was bought, demolished and a set of wrought iron gates put up leading to the gardens. Seating and flower beds were also laid down. The gardens remain a tranquil place where people often go to sit and reflect.

The end of the war was celebrated in grand style in Harborough with joyous street parties held under blissfully warm sunshine. Celebratory parades marched through the town on VE Day on 13 May 1945. The salute was taken at the (now-disappeared) roundabout next to the Peacock and the Cock Inn. On 24 August 1945 the 'Harborough Mail' carried a double-page spread about the jubilant celebrations for VJ Day. Huge crowds had gathered in Welland Park to share the moment and more street parties were held, organised by the 'ladies in the streets' according to Mail reports. There was dancing all night in Welland Park, around the bandstand, and the Town Band gave a concert. Eight years later, in 1953, there was more dancing in the streets to celebrate the Coronation of Queen Elizabeth II.

Twenty-five years later, in June 1977, there would be more patriotic celebrations to mark the Queen's Silver Jubilee. The many street parties, including a huge one in Wartnaby Street, which took place in the town reflected a strong support for the monarchy. Harborough was decorated by two-and-a-half miles of red, white and blue bunting made by residents of Care Village Shangton and put up by members of the Round Table. In Sibbertoft near Harborough they celebrated the Silver Jubilee with a football match where the married men of the village played the single men and won 4-2 respectively.

Because of a major shortage of housing in Harborough immediately after the war, the council found itself facing a new

Did you know?

Post War Housing Boom

In the 25 years after the end of the Second World War, more than 2,000 houses were built in Harborough.

problem - squatting - and needed to take steps to alleviate the situation. Among those employed on the new building - initially on land that was being used as lairage opposite the station and land to the south-west of the town - were prisoners of war. Housing sprang up in what became Meadow Street, the Headlands and the Broadway, accessible when Roman Way was opened up. Then work began on the Southern Estate that was to accommodate 700 houses, supported by an infrastructure of shops and amenities. As building materials became more readily available other estates followed at Rectory Lane, Highfield and Fairlawn. The Shropshire Close flats were built and the Bowden Lane flats known as Oxford House were built for the elderly. In recent years, Oxford House became very run-down, and has been rebuilt, as two new flats Goddard Court and Matthew Clarke House.

In the 1950s, the town celebrated a huge sporting achievement and had a new hero to toast. Harborough-born boxer, Jack Gardner, described by one of his brothers as 'the perfect specimen of man', represented Great Britain in the 1948 London Olympics and reached the very height of his sport in 1950 when he gained three major boxing titles.

There has been a long tradition of boxing greats in Harborough - Reggie Meen, British heavyweight champion 1931-32 and George Aldridge, British middleweight champion 1963-64, as well as Jack Gardner.

Jack and his two younger brothers Bob and Rod were all boxers. It had been their father Len's dream to see one of his sons win an army boxing title, just as he had done. Not only did two of the brothers win army titles but, in 1950 his son Jack beat Doncaster boxer Bruce Woodcock at London's White City Stadium to become British, British Empire and European Heavyweight Boxing Champion. He held all three titles for two years.

It was a supremely proud moment for Jack's father and for the people of Market Harborough. Jack's brother Rod Gardner, who grew up with his family in Cross Street,

recalls: 'When we were young, we set up a boxing club in the yard of the Peacock. The trainer there was a chap called Fred Pollard'. Fred had boxed in his youth but was forced to give it up because, ironically, although he had never received a serious injury in the boxing ring, he was blinded in one eye while playing cricket when a ball hit him in the face. The brothers sparred with each other at the club during training. During one sparring session, Rod Gardner ended up with a broken jaw from a punch delivered by his brother Bob. Later, the brothers had to head down to London to compete in amateur boxing matches because there were very few people boxing in the Midlands.

After Jack's great triumph, a celebratory dinner was held for him in the Assembly Rooms in Harborough. Jack died in 1980, aged 54. You can see a plaque commemorating him on a bench in front of the Old Grammar School. There is also a hall at Harborough Leisure Centre named after him.

Did you know?

The Citizens Cup

The first person to be awarded the Citizens Cup, given to individuals who had distinguished themselves in Harborough, was butcher H H Pickering (see chapter two). Boxer Jack Gardner also held the cup for a time. It was also awarded to organisations such as the Archaeological Society and St John Ambulance Brigade.

FLOODS

THE TOWN FLOODED 1958   ZZZ01041 (Reproduced thanks to Andrew Carpenter and 'Harborough Mail')

This famous photograph, which hangs in the reception of the 'Harborough Mail', shows the paper's then editor Ken Hankins and reporter Bob Hemingway in the Square up to their waists in flood water.

Harborough has always been prone to floods. There had been several severe floods in the town during the war, but the 'worst of the century', as the Harborough Mail reported, hit on 2 July 1958 when thousands of pounds worth of damage was caused as water levels rose to nearly five feet in the early hours smashing plate-glass shop windows around the Square under the pressure of the water. Not everyone had a bad time in the floods - youngsters had the excuse to ask for rides across the Square in council dustcarts to avoid getting wet.

After this the council launched schemes for future flood relief. The riverbed was deepened and widened and new bridges were built to allow a greater flow of water beneath them. Work was also carried out on the River Jordan in Little Bowden.

Nevertheless, in 2002 and 2004 several major flash floods hit Harborough causing thousands of pounds worth of damage to shops and businesses and prompted the start of a flood alleviation project that has slowly been put in place by Anglian Water. This will involve increasing the size of Folly Pond. Only time will tell if it's successful.

THE SQUARE AND HIGH STREET c1965   M33045t

Did you know?

Market Harborough Drama Society

Formed in 1933, the Market Harborough Drama Society had no permanent venue until 1962. Prior to that they performed in a number of different buildings, particularly the Assembly Rooms in Abbey Street, now the Golden Wonder offices. In 1962 they acquired the Green Dragon Inn, which had been the priest's house in the Middle Ages. At first the lower floor of the building was still being used as a garage and bike shed for Symington's workers. Eventually they converted it all into a small theatre, later to be known as Harborough Theatre.

The Square and High Street

THE SQUARE LOOKING NORTH c1950 M33504

The people casually holding a conversation in the middle of the road would be risking their lives today. The Old Crown Inn and the Cock Inn no longer exist - they now house Bairstow Eves and Viyella, respectively.

THE SQUARE AND HIGH STREET c1965 M33045

The roundabouts were introduced in 1937 as part of a reorganisation of the Square. They no longer exist.

THE SQUARE c1955 M33016

THE SQUARE c1950 M33501p

The posts around the war memorial were to protect it from buses, back when the Square was used as a bus stop.

THE SQUARE c1965 M33075

THE SQUARE c1965 M33063p

In the 1960s the car reigned supreme! How things have changed for the better - the area was pedestrianised in the 1970s and parking moved to the Commons Car Park.

HIGH STREET c1965 M33094

The Sugar Loaf pub has replaced the Mac Fisheries shop, Woolworth's to its right is now Savers and Barclays replaced the former Stamford, Spalding and Boston Bank. The chemist on the left is now Peacocks.

HIGH STREET c1965   M33094

THE SQUARE c1965   M33063p

In 1974 Harborough District Council was created when the Market Harborough Urban District Council and the Rural Districts of Harborough, Billesdon and Lutterworth were merged. Harborough District Council elected 37 councillors and, for the first time, the council became a planning authority, taking over powers previously administered by the county council. Today Harborough District Council's motto is 'Good practice and innovation in the heart of rural England'.

For many years district councillors and campaigners had unsuccessfully tried to block Home Office plans to expand the existing prison, a former Polish refugee camp, just outside Harborough, near Lubenham. The prison, namely Gartree, which holds prisoners serving life sentences, would come to witness some of the most dramatic events in the town's history. In November 1972, some of the country's most notorious criminals were involved in riots at the prison and five prisoners were found trying to escape from the maximum-security wing during the chaos.

In October 1978, nearly 250 prisoners took control of three blocks of Gartree for more than 12 hours. All 200 of the prison's staff and warders from other jails, including Liverpool, were drafted in wearing protective riot gear to help cope with the situation. They were joined by 150 policemen and an expert team of marksmen. The riot ended the following day when a compromise was reached and rioters agreed to talk to senior prison officers.

In December 1987, the prison hit the national headlines again when a daring helicopter sky bust helped two dangerous convicts escape. The daytime jailbreak, the first of its kind in the UK, took prison staff completely by surprise. It took only 30 seconds to lift killer Sydney Draper and gang boss John Kendall to freedom when a hijacked helicopter landed in the exercise yard of the prison. Kendall and Draper made a dash for the helicopter while fellow inmates held back prison officers. Kendall was caught within weeks, but Draper eluded re-capture for 14 months.

Did you know?
Gartree

The name of Gartree dates back to ancient times when criminals were executed by hanging at the Gallow-tree in the parish, just outside Harborough. This was a 'tree of justice' where criminals would 'take leave of this world'. Over time, the name 'gallow-tree' slowly became 'Gar-tree'. It is fitting that it should now be the site of a prison that, incidentally, was built in Gallowfield Road.

In January 1978 a devastating fire ripped through the Tungstone Batteries factory in Lathkill Street, causing an estimated £1million worth of damage. It was the biggest fire Harborough had seen for years and was caused by an electrical fault. Although the incident happened during a fire-fighters strike, crews did leave the picket lines to tackle the blaze.

Harborough Museum opened in Adam and Eve Street in 1983 and began putting together a collection of artefacts dating back to 1932 collected by the Market Harborough Historical Society. The museum is now poised to go into a period of major expansion.

Also in 1983, the Department of Transport unveiled options for Harborough's A6 bypass to a storm of controversy about safety. Finally, five years and a public inquiry later the preferred option of a four-and-a-half mile road skirting past the nearby village of Great Bowden was chosen. The project was to cause a period of major disruption in the town.

The Ritz

THE RITZ, NORTHAMPTON ROAD c1955 M33020

In 1978, the Ritz cinema in Northampton Road closed. It had been built in 1939 and had always been a favourite. Bands even used to play on top of its entrance, in a style reminiscent of the Beatles' rooftop gig. Considered expensive when it first opened, it's ironic that it is now a Kwik Save supermarket.

Leisure Centre

LEISURE CENTRE 2004 ZZZ01067

In 1990, Harborough's much-needed and long-awaited leisure centre was built. A leisure centre project had actually been agreed in principle as far back as 1981, but councillors spent a decade wondering where to build it - Welland Park, Symington's Recreation Ground and the old cattle market were among other places originally mooted until a site at Northampton Road was chosen. The centre cost £3 million and houses a swimming pool (replacing the old swimming baths in Northampton Road), a gym and indoor and outdoor sports pitches. It later gained an indoor bowls centre and the 'air dome' covered sports hall. During the leisure centre's grand opening, in the presence of a host of dignitaries, the water suddenly turned black due to a problem with the filter! It was soon back on track though and given the royal seal of approval by Princess Anne.

During the 1990s the town witnessed some of the most dramatic changes its people had ever seen, as did Little Bowden and Great Bowden. It also saw some of the worst ever disruption, caused when the town centre was quite literally dug up as part of the Bypass Demonstration Project.

A number of major construction projects seemed to coincide creating a chaotic couple of years in the town. They included work on the sewer works, the town enhancement, the development of St Mary's Place and the moving of the cattle market to Lubenham. This was followed by traffic calming measures, part of the Bypass Demonstration Project, which started in Fairfield Road and spread to other areas of the town the following year. The 'Inner Gateway' was also created at the Leicester Road entrance to the town as part of the safety measures whereby the road was narrowed and traffic was effectively 'squeezed' to ensure slower speeds.

Harborough had been chosen as one of six towns to benefit from the Bypass Demonstration Project whereby the town would receive extra funding once the new bypass was opened. But for two years, between 1993 and 1995, Harborough became one big construction area and people began to wonder where all these benefits were. Armies of JCBs, trucks and workmen descended on the town and began ripping it up. The construction work hit traders extremely hard because the town centre, with its seemingly relentless noise and disruption, was not an environment compatible with the leisurely shopper. Radio reports were even warning shoppers not to venture into Harborough because of the road works. Rising out of the chaos was the St Mary's Place shopping centre, built at the same time and replacing the old cattle market. While some viewed it as a modern blot on the landscape, it brought in much-needed new chain stores and regenerated the southern part of the town centre.

The two years of upheaval devastated the town, so much so that in September 1995 a day of celebration was organised in the town

> ## Did you know?
>
> *St Mary's Place was officially opened by Ken Morley, Reg Holdsworth from Coronation Street, and the stars of the Batman and Robin TV series.*

celebrate the end of the roadworks. The subsequent benefits that the redevelopment brought to Harborough in terms of its economy and the overall look of the town, made those dark two years of chaos worth it and set the town up for its grand entrance into the new millennium.

THE SQUARE UNDER CONSTRUCTION 1993-95 ZZZ01040 (Photo by Andrew Carpenter).

What a sight! Who can forget the upheaval of the early 1990s?

CHAPTER FIVE

A New Millennium

ARTS FRESCO ZZZ01028

ARTS FRESCO ZZZ01029

THOSE WHO live in Harborough today live in a town adapting to a rapidly changing modern age, whilst retaining the character of a much-loved traditional market town.

This is no mean feat. In recent times, Market Harborough has enjoyed a boom period. This boom has led to an increasing demand for services and facilities. Thus the town's schools, organisations, shops and societies have grown and will continue to grow if this trend continues.

The town now boasts a healthy population of more than 18,500 people. It has become a highly sought after place to live - reflected in the ever-increasing house prices! Houses in Harborough are now more than two-and-a-half times more expensive than they were ten years ago, with an average house price of a staggering £185,000. Part of the reason for this is the town's prime location on the commuter belt. Improvements in the railways, particularly in the last decade, have made it possible to travel from Market Harborough to London in just over an hour rather than the 90 minutes it used to take. The introduction of the super-fast Midland Mainline Turbostar trains doubled the number of passengers over-night. When the Turbostar is replaced by the Meridian service the line will be fast and promises to have improved internal décor as well. Once London's St Pancras station is linked to the Channel Tunnel line people will be able to jump on a train at Harborough Station and travel across Europe, ending up in Belgium just a few hours later.

The town also sits within easy reach of the A14 between the east coast and the M1 and M6 motorways, making the town very appealing to people who work in big cities such as London, Leicester or Nottingham but want to come back each night to a town that feels homely and safe. Leicestershire and, in particular, Market Harborough are officially some of the safest places to live in the country in terms of crime. Perhaps because of this, a new trend is emerging whereby Londoners living south of the River Thames are selling their homes in the capital for massive sums and buying a very similar house in Market Harborough for half the price. That's because Market Harborough has a sense of community unlike anywhere else. Living in Harborough, compared to London, arguably brings with it a better quality of life, with better health and education.

Thus there is a new breed of resident in Market Harborough. One hundred and thirty years ago rapid housing expansion produced a New Harborough; perhaps now those who move to the town and commute to work elsewhere could be termed New Harborians.

Did you know?

Harborough Bricks used in St Pancras Station

Thousands of Harborough bricks, dug and fired locally, were used to help build London's St Pancras station.

CARNIVAL ZZZ01024

These people have made Harborough their home and feel very much a part of its community. There are cynics, of course, who will argue that an influx of outsiders, who use the town merely as a commuting base, will find it difficult to establish themselves in the community. But if they are willing, the opportunities are here to add something to the town, thus ensuring Harborough's strong sense of community is not lost. Harborough is a welcoming town and it does not take long to feel a part of it, even as an outsider. It is certainly true that you frequently meet people who will regale you with tales of how they only moved here because of a job, but ended up starting a family or retiring here. People choose to stay in the town for the strangest reasons. I remember one woman telling me how, while house hunting around Warwickshire and Leicestershire with her family, they stumbled upon Harborough on carnival day. They all decided there and then that they wanted to live in Market Harborough. They now do, and in fact went on to help organise the town's carnival event.

The town's attractions are vast and varied, hence its continued growth with the development of new housing estates pushing the boundaries of Harborough ever further. Streets you may live in yourself such as Ashley Way, Alvington Way, Farndale View or the Brookfield development are just a few examples of housing built to accommodate the town's new intake. These new estates are, arguably, the New Harborough of today, reminiscent of the rapid housing developments of the 19th century. There are, perhaps, some who feel that these swathes of new development could impinge on the character of the town, but this is yet to happen. In fact, it is a testament to the integrity of our councillors and Harborough District Council's planning committees over the past 30 years that Market Harborough has retained its character and not been swamped with ugly, modern developments. It has to be said though that Harborough's new struggle will be in adapting to meet the needs of an increasing population, while respecting the opinions of those who have lived in the town for many years and may resist overt changes.

Did you know?
Missing House Numbers

What happened to the missing house numbers in Great Bowden Road? When houses were springing up in the street, the builders left gaps in house numbers so that more houses or flats could be added behind the existing homes at a later date. But many of these were never built, so the house numbers remain missing!

A New Millennium

IN THE PARK c1950 M33505
The River Welland, along which the magnificent Millennium Mile was created.

On 8 January 2000 the Millennium Mile - a beautiful walk and cycle way along the River Welland - was opened by the people of the town. The idea to mark the town's move into the 21st century in this way was put forward by a Harborough school pupil. It is enjoyed by scores of walkers and cyclists every day, as is the whole of the Welland Valley around Harborough, which has become a haven for ramblers and keen cyclists.

Market Harborough
U3A Millennium Tapestry

MILLENNIUM TAPESTRY ZZZ01026

Harborough's rich historical tapestry was also celebrated at the turn of the millennium with exactly that - a rich historical tapestry. The Market Harborough University of the Third Age (U3A) designed and crafted a stunning woven tapestry depicting the town's history and present day features. Measuring 2.9m wide by 1.6m high, it took three-and-a-half years to complete and brilliantly captures the personality of Harborough. It can be seen in the town library.

In 2004 Market Harborough celebrated its 800th anniversary as a market town. The district council marked the occasion by unveiling plans to redesign a number of street nameplates.

The town's local newspaper the 'Harborough Mail' also celebrated a birthday - its 150th. As well as entertaining and informing on a weekly basis, the newspaper continues to champion the people of the town. Recently the newspaper launched a successful campaign to help bring much-needed NHS dentists to Harborough. It took the spirited campaign to Downing Street, even sending a dossier about the dental crisis to the Prime Minister. The paper's letters page, which remains crammed with people's views on any number of controversial issues, reflects how strongly its readers feel about their town.

No issue is controversial unless people care about it. It is this fierce sense of pride and a depth of feeling about what goes on in the town, that makes Harborough what it is today. Community and social events in the town continue to thrive. The town's annual carnival goes from strength to strength, attracting thousands of revellers and raising thousands of pounds for charity every year. The festive Late Night Shopping event, which has been held every December since 1987, also helps raise vital funds for charity as well as providing a major boost for local shops and businesses.

More than 40 years after it found a permanent venue, Market Harborough Drama Society continues to produce sell-out shows at Harborough Theatre. The society stages six plays a year, each running for a week. There are now plans in the pipeline to raise £400,000 to expand Harborough Theatre and widen resources. Neighbouring premises have already been bought and planning permission for the extension has been approved. In an age when Harborough Theatre is competing against such things as DVDs, the internet and computer games for entertainment, any news of Harborough expanding its cultural output, through its theatre or anything else, must be wholeheartedly welcomed. If Harborough could fully cater for its own community's cultural and artistic tastes as well as regularly attracting audiences from much further afield, it would be a remarkable achievement.

In conclusion, history has been kind to the town. It has blessed it with some unique and spectacular focal points. It is a town with a strong sense of community spirit that we are reminded of every day. It is a community that is never stronger than in times of celebration such as the happy and glorious Golden Jubilee parties or in times of grief, such as

MARKET HARBOROUGH TODAY ZZZ01056

Flower power came to town recently when, after several years of trying, Harborough scooped the prestigious East Midlands in Bloom title two years in a row. Harborough added to its success by winning a bronze medal in the Britain in Bloom finals.

Rugby Ace

Recently, the town has produced a World Cup winner, rugby ace Martin Johnson. The England, British Lions and Leicester Tigers skipper, who attended Ridgeway Primary School, Welland Park Community College and the Robert Smyth School, lifted the Webb Ellis Cup in 2003. He captained the courageous England rugby team to victory in that unforgettably dramatic World Cup final against Australia. He has since published a best-selling autobiography and continues to make guest appearances at events in his hometown.

MARTIN JOHNSON ZZZ01030
(Photograph by Andrew Carpenter)

when candles were lit in the parish church for the victims of the World Trade Center tragedy in New York.

We are indebted to the thousands of traders, business people, architects, councillors and characters who have been responsible for shaping the town over the years. We owe it to them to continue to make our town great. How it develops will, to some extent, be affected by national changes, perhaps even international changes. But it is a certainty that the people living in Harborough, those living at the grass-roots level, will be involved somehow. It is taken as read, that Harborians will continue to feel proud of their town and fight for what they believe is right for it.

Villages around Harborough, while retaining their own independence, will continue to look to the town for guidance and strong administrative leadership. It is not possible to predict the future, but it is certain that the modern changes and technology we are dazzled by today will one day seem old fashioned. We can only imagine how things develop.

Market Harborough is a thriving town with a rich history for future generations to build on and a town to be proud of.

As for the future, well, that's over to you.

VICTORIAN COUNTY MAP OF LEICESTERSHIRE FEATURING MARKET HARBOROUGH c1850

BIBLIOGRAPHY

Town Affairs: The Making of Modern Market Harborough - J C Davies,
Market Harborough Urban District Council
The Beginnings of Market Harborough - David Crouch, Institute of Historical Research
Around Market Harborough - Steph Mastoris, Alan Sutton Publishing
Bowden to Harborough - J C Davies, Wellandside Photographics Ltd
Fifteen Years of the Local Board - W B Bragg, published by G Green.
District of Harborough: Official Guide - British Publishing Company Ltd
Bygone Days in Market Harborough - John Bland, Green & Co Booksellers
Market Harborough: As I Remember It - Jane Burrows, Leicestershire Libraries
Victorian Harborough - J C Davies & Michael C Brown, Barracuda Books
Georgian Harborough - J C Davies, Wellandside Photographics Ltd
The Harborough Area in Old Picture Postcards - Pam Aucott & Steph Mastoris, European Library
Bygone Market Harborough - John Anderson, published by John Anderson
Market Harborough U3A Millennium Tapestry - Anne Allen and Jane Burrows,
designed and produced by Travelsphere Ltd
Harborough in Camera - Pam Aucott & Steph Mastoris, Alan Sutton Publishing
Naseby 1645-1995, A 350th Anniversary Souvenir - Andrew Holmes,
published by Harborough Mail
Market Harborough, A Photographic History of Your Town, Stephen Barker,
Black Horse Books for WH Smith
Leicestershire Architects - J D Bennett, Leicestershire County Council

ACKNOWLEDGEMENTS

Harborough Mail, Harborough Museum, Bob Hakewill, Rosalind Willatts, Jane Tugwell,
George Pickering, Cedric Ashton, Philip Dearing, Rod Gardner, Nick Lewis, James Briggs,
Harborough Library, Harborough District Council, Leicester Mercury, The Civic Society,
Leicestershire County Council Heritage Services,
The Courtaulds Group, Symingtons, Kathryn Allen

Francis Frith
Pioneer Victorian Photographer

Francis Frith, founder of the world-famous photographic archive, was a multi-talented man. A devout Quaker and a highly successful Victorian businessman, he was philosophical by nature and pioneering in outlook. By 1855 he had already established a wholesale grocery business in Liverpool, and sold it for the astonishing sum of £200,000, which is the equivalent today of over £15,000,000. Now in his thirties, and captivated by the new science of photography, Frith set out on a series of pioneering journeys up the Nile and to the Near East.

He was the first photographer to venture beyond the sixth cataract of the Nile. Africa was still the mysterious 'Dark Continent', and Stanley and Livingstone's historic meeting was a decade into the future. The conditions for picture taking confound belief. He laboured for hours in his wicker dark-room in the sweltering heat of the desert, while the volatile chemicals fizzed dangerously in their trays. Back in London he exhibited his photographs and was 'rapturously cheered' by members of the Royal Society. His reputation as a photographer was made overnight.

By the 1870s the railways had threaded their way across the country, and Bank Holidays and half-day Saturdays had been made obligatory by Act of Parliament. All of a sudden the working man and his family were able to enjoy days out, take holidays, and see a little more of the world.

With typical business acumen, Francis Frith foresaw that these new tourists would enjoy having souvenirs to commemorate their days out. For the next thirty years he travelled the country by train and by pony and trap, producing fine photographs of seaside resorts and beauty spots that were keenly bought by millions of Victorians. These prints were painstakingly pasted into family albums and pored over during the dark nights of winter, rekindling precious memories of summer excursions. Frith's studio was soon supplying retail shops all over the country, and by 1890 F Frith & Co had become the greatest specialist photographic publishing company in the world, with over 2,000 sales outlets, and pioneered the picture postcard.

Francis Frith had died in 1898 at his villa in Cannes, his great project still growing. By 1970 the archive he created contained over a third of a million pictures showing 7,000 British towns and villages.

Frith's legacy to us today is of immense significance and value, for the magnificent archive of evocative photographs he created provides a unique record of change in the cities, towns and villages throughout Britain over a century and more. Frith and his fellow studio photographers revisited locations many times down the years to update their views, compiling for us an enthralling and colourful pageant of British life and character.

We are fortunate that Frith was dedicated to recording the minutiae of everyday life. For it is this sheer wealth of visual data, the painstaking chronicle of changes in dress, transport, street layouts, buildings, housing and landscape that captivates us so much today, offering us a powerful link with the past and with the lives of our ancestors.

Computers have now made it possible for Frith's many thousands of images to be accessed almost instantly. The archive offers every one of us an opportunity to examine the places where we and our families have lived and worked down the years. Its images, depicting our shared past, are now bringing pleasure and enlightenment to millions around the world a century and more after his death. For further information visit: **www.francisfrith.com**

FRITH PRODUCTS & SERVICES

Francis Frith would doubtless be pleased to know that the pioneering publishing venture he started in 1860 still continues today. Over a hundred and forty years later, The Francis Frith Collection continues in the same innovative tradition and is now one of the foremost publishers of vintage photographs in the world. Some of the current activities include:

INTERIOR DECORATION

Today Frith's photographs can be seen framed and as giant wall murals in thousands of pubs, restaurants, hotels, banks, retail stores and other public buildings throughout the country. In every case they enhance the unique local atmosphere of the places they depict and provide reminders of gentler days in an increasingly busy and frenetic world.

PRODUCT PROMOTIONS

Frith products are used by many major companies to promote the sales of their own products or to reinforce their own history and heritage. Frith promotions have been used by Hovis bread, Courage beers, Scots Porage Oats, Colman's mustard, Cadbury's foods, Mellow Birds coffee, Dunhill pipe tobacco, Guinness, and Bulmer's Cider.

GENEALOGY AND FAMILY HISTORY

As the interest in family history and roots grows world-wide, more and more people are turning to Frith's photographs of Great Britain for images of the towns, villages and streets where their ancestors lived; and, of course, photographs of the churches and chapels where their ancestors were christened, married and buried are an essential part of every genealogy tree and family album.

FRITH PRODUCTS

All Frith photographs are available Framed or just as Mounted Prints and Posters (size 23 x 16 inches). These may be ordered from the address below. Other products available are - Address Books, Calendars, Jigsaws, Canvas Prints, Postcards and local and prestige books.

THE INTERNET

Already ninety thousand Frith photographs can be viewed and purchased on the internet through the Frith websites and a myriad of partner sites.

For more detailed information on Frith products, look at this site:
www.francisfrith.com

See the complete list of Frith Books at: www.francisfrith.com
This web site is regularly updated with the latest list of publications from The Francis Frith Collection. If you wish to buy books relating to another part of the country that your local bookshop does not stock, you may purchase on-line.

For further information, trade, or author enquiries please contact us at the address below:
The Francis Frith Collection, Unit 6, Oakley Business Park, Wylye Road, Dinton, Wiltshire SP3 5EU.
Tel: +44 (0)1722 716 376 Fax: +44 (0)1722 716 881 Email: sales@francisfrith.co.uk

---

See Frith products on the internet at www.francisfrith.com

FREE PRINT OF YOUR CHOICE
CHOOSE A PHOTOGRAPH FROM THIS BOOK
+ £3.50 POSTAGE

Mounted Print
Overall size 14 x 11 inches (355 x 280mm)

TO RECEIVE YOUR FREE PRINT

Choose any Frith photograph in this book

Simply complete the Voucher opposite and return it with your remittance for £3.50 (to cover postage and handling) and we will print the photograph of your choice in SEPIA (size 11 x 8 inches) and supply it in a cream mount ready to frame (overall size 14 x 11 inches).

Order additional Mounted Prints
at HALF PRICE - £12.00 each (normally £24.00)

If you would like to order more Frith prints from this book, possibly as gifts for friends and family, you can buy them at half price (with no additional postage costs).

Have your Mounted Prints framed

For an extra £20.00 per print you can have your mounted print(s) framed in an elegant polished wood and gilt moulding, overall size 16 x 13 inches (no additional postage required).

IMPORTANT!

❶ Please note: aerial photographs and photographs with a reference number starting with a "Z" are not Frith photographs and cannot be supplied under this offer.

❷ Offer valid for delivery to one UK address only.

❸ These special prices are only available if you use this form to order. You must use the ORIGINAL VOUCHER on this page (no copies permitted). We can only despatch to one UK address.

❹ This offer cannot be combined with any other offer.

As a customer your name & address will be stored by Frith but not sold or rented to third parties. Your data will be used for the purpose of this promotion only.

Send completed Voucher form to:
The Francis Frith Collection,
6 Oakley Business Park, Wylye Road,
Dinton, Wiltshire SP3 5EU

Voucher for *FREE* and Reduced Price *Frith Prints*

Please do not photocopy this voucher. Only the original is valid, so please fill it in, cut it out and return it to us with your order.

Picture ref no	Page no	Qty	Mounted @ £12.00	Framed + £20.00	Total Cost £
		1	Free of charge*	£	£
			£12.00	£	£
			£12.00	£	£
			£12.00	£	£
			£12.00	£	£
			£12.00	£	£

Please allow 28 days for delivery. Offer available to one UK address only

* Post & handling		£3.80
Total Order Cost		£

Title of this book . . . .

I enclose a cheque/postal order for £ . . . . made payable to 'The Francis Frith Collection'

OR please debit my Mastercard / Visa / Maestro card, details below

Card Number:

Issue No (Maestro only):   Valid from (Maestro):

Card Security Number: Expires:

Signature:

Name Mr/Mrs/Ms ....

Address ....

....

....

.... Postcode ....

Daytime Tel No ....

Email ....

Valid to 31/12/15

Can you help us with information about any of the Frith photographs in this book?

We are gradually compiling an historical record for each of the photographs in the Frith archive. It is always fascinating to find out the names of the people shown in the pictures, as well as insights into the shops, buildings and other features depicted.

If you recognize anyone in the photographs in this book, or if you have information not already included in the author's caption, do let us know. We would love to hear from you, and will try to publish it in future books or articles.

An Invitation from The Francis Frith Collection to Share Your Memories

The 'Share Your Memories' feature of our website allows members of the public to add personal memories relating to the places featured in our photographs, or comment on others already added. Seeing a place from your past can rekindle forgotten or long held memories. Why not visit the website, find photographs of places you know well and add YOUR story for others to read and enjoy? We would love to hear from you!

www.francisfrith.com/memories

Our production team

Frith books are produced by a small dedicated team at offices near Salisbury. Most have worked with the Frith Collection for many years. All have in common one quality: they have a passion for the Frith Collection.

Frith Books and Gifts

We have a wide range of books and gifts available on our website utilising our photographic archive, many of which can be individually personalised.

www.francisfrith.com